D1254082

Pre-Algebra Step-by-Step

—— Introduction ——

*P*re-Algebra Step-by-Step is a book with a wide variety of uses. Middle school students will enjoy using this book to begin to learn the basics of algebra. Those who have already had an introduction to algebra will find the activities helpful in reinforcing what they have learned. Students who are already taking pre-algebra, but find it too much of a struggle, can use this book to gain the additional support they need in order to succeed.

Each chapter provides basic information. Students are taken through the world of algebra step-by-step. The activities are written so that students may be successful on their own without any additional instruction as long as they have a firm foundation in basic math. Reinforcement and practice suggestions are given at the beginning of each chapter for teachers to use with students.

Even though the material covered in this book is very basic, students are also challenged. Students are asked questions that challenge them to think about what they are doing and why the procedures work. The author does not promote rote memorization of processes. Instead, students learn by discovery and understanding.

If your students seem concerned about when they will use the math they are required to learn, they won't have to worry about that while using the materials contained in *Pre-Algebra Step-by-Step*. Every chapter includes applications of algebra that are relevant and meaningful to students.

Tools of the Trade
Teaching Notes

Concerning any topic, there are tools involved that are understood only by those who possess a knowledge of that topic. The same is true for the many branches of mathematics. Each branch comes with its own set of "tools"—symbols, jargon, properties, and rules of protocol. This chapter introduces students to the tools necessary for them to experience success in pre-algebra.

Some of the material in this chapter may be a review for students. Some tools are discussed in relation to other branches of mathematics. Students must be more than familiar with these tools before they can attempt other algebraic skills. This is the time for true mastery. The activities provided may be used to assess students' mastery of each type of tool.

If some students find it difficult to remember all the tools, you may want to consider the following extension activities.

"Tools" Bingo
This activity can be used if students just need a little more practice with the tools. Have each student create a bingo card which they will swap with a friend. In each of the cells on the card, the student should write one of the tools covered in this chapter.

After students swap cards, start off the game by writing an example of any of the tools covered in this chapter on the chalkboard or overhead. As always with bingo, only those students who have that specific tool on their cards may cover it. Ask a student to give the next example. This student is not allowed to give as an example a tool that would cause him or her to get a bingo in that turn. Continue the game with students giving examples until someone calls "bingo." The student who calls "bingo" should go to the board and match up the tools with the examples needed to make the bingo. If the student is correct, the game is over and that student is declared the winner. If the matches are not made correctly, continue the game until another student calls "bingo."

"Tools" Manual
This activity is meant for those students who need more concentrated work on the tools. As an individual or a group assignment, have students make a tools manual. Each page of the manual should contain one of the tools, its definition or use, an example of its use, and a memory aid. The memory aid can be a humorous drawing or saying, or it could be a way to link the tool to previous knowledge.

If this is done as a group activity, each group could be responsible for one set of tools. The completed class manual should be available at all times for students to use as a reference.

Symbols

When working with pre-algebra, you will notice a few new symbols. Some of the symbols with which you are familiar (i.e. +, -, >, etc.) are used just as they always have been. But a few new symbols are necessary. The next few pages are meant to get you acquainted with these symbols so that they will not be so foreign when you see them. If you should forget what a symbol means, you can always return to these pages to help you remember.

Multiplication

There are alternate ways of noting the operation of multiplication. Since letters of the alphabet are used quite a bit in algebra, the more familiar symbol for multiplication (x) could be misinterpreted as the letter x. So other notation options were devised. The notations for multiplication are shown below.

$$a \times b$$
$$a \cdot b$$
$$ab \text{ or } a(b)$$

Concerning the last option, parentheses are used only when numbers are being multiplied, such as 5(6), since the lack of parentheses would make it seem like just a single number, 56.

Comparison

In your first years of school, you learned to use the "less than" and "greater than" symbols, < and >. These symbols are used again in algebra. In addition, a few more related symbols join them.

<	less than
>	greater than
≤	less than or equal to
≥	greater than or equal to
≠	not equal to
≈	approximately equal to

When using the ≤ or ≥ symbols, the values on either side of the symbol can be equal, or one can be greater than the other. The following are all true statements.

$$5 < 7$$
$$5 > 4$$
$$5 \leq 19$$
$$5 \geq 5$$
$$5 \neq 11$$
$$5.99 \approx 6$$

Symbols continued

Absolute Value

Absolute value is indicated by two vertical bars. |3| is read as "the absolute value of three." Absolute value is a way of ensuring that an answer is positive, rather than negative. This is useful when you are dealing with things that cannot be negative, such as distance or time. Any number within absolute value bars is made positive before the absolute value bars are removed. Just as with parentheses, all the calculating is done before the bars are removed. Below are a few examples.

$$|3| = 3$$
$$|-3| = 3$$
$$|6 + 4| = |10| = 10$$
$$|17 - 6| = |11| = 11$$

Repeating Decimals

Some decimal numbers continue indefinitely. For example, look at the fraction ⅓. You may remember that a fraction can be changed to a decimal by dividing the denominator (the bottom number) into the numerator (the top number).

$$
\begin{array}{r}
0.3333\ldots \\
3\overline{)1.0000} \\
\underline{9} \\
10 \\
\underline{9} \\
10 \\
\underline{9} \\
1
\end{array}
$$

You can see that this will continue forever. So, ⅓ = 0.3333 . . .

Instead of using ". . ." to signify that a decimal continues forever, mathematicians draw a bar over the part of the decimal that continues.

$$⅓ = 0.\overline{3}$$

Here are a few more examples:

$$0.41414141\ldots = 0.\overline{41}$$
$$6.6666\ldots = 6.\overline{6}$$
$$17.1544444\ldots = 17.15\overline{4}$$
$$0.142857142857142857\ldots = 0.\overline{142857}$$

Symbols Practice

Make the following number sentences true by filling in the appropriate symbols. The missing symbols can be any of those described in this section.

1. 5 6 = 30

2. 467   16

3. 67   72

4. -4   4

5. 87.995   88

6. 14 47 = 658

7. 92 > 92

8. 14.141141 . . . = 14.141

9. 45 = 9 5

10. 620   620

11. 56.143 = 56.143143143

12. 33   42

Complete the following number sentences.

13. 5.16516516 . . . = _____

14. 27.9912 ≈ _____

15. |47 − 32| = _____

16. 34.6 ≥ _____

17. 91 ≤ _____

18. |-52| = _____

19. |17 − 38| = _____

20. 582.9939 ≈ _____

21. 43 < _____

22. |32| = _____

The Number Maze

Make a path through the maze below to the exit. Follow the pathways that hold numbers that correctly complete the number sentence.

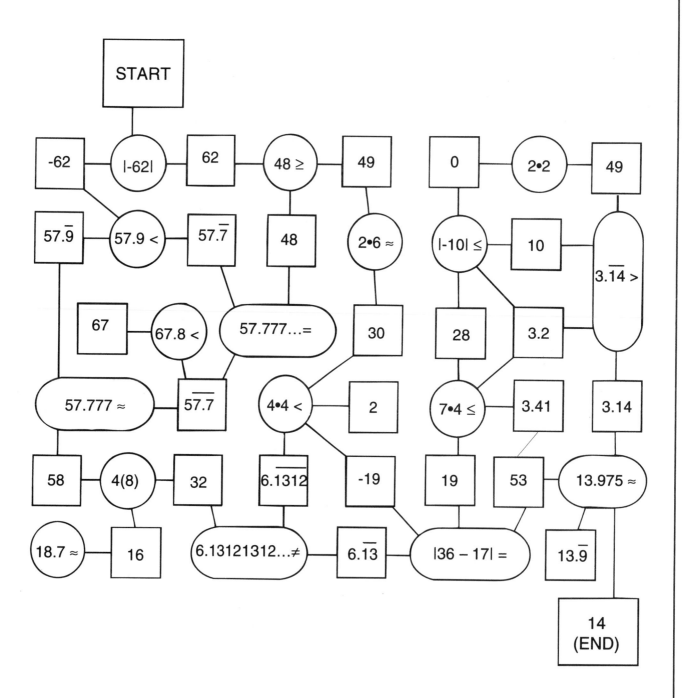

Numbers

The business of mathematics is, for the most part, working with numbers. There are many different types of numbers. There are whole numbers, decimals, fractions, etc. The set of numbers you use most frequently is probably the set of whole numbers. In some cases, it is important to know the type of number with which you are dealing.

Below and on page 7 are descriptions of the sets of numbers you will primarily work with in algebra. Along with each description is a handy memory aid. Use it to help you remember each set of numbers and its unique attributes.

Natural Numbers
These are also called "counting numbers." When you start counting, you begin with 1 and proceed increasing by one each time. So, remembering that natural numbers are simply the numbers you use when you count, you'll never forget that this set is:

$$\{1, 2, 3, 4, 5, 6, \ldots \}$$

Whole Numbers
This set of numbers is closely related to the set of natural numbers. Instead of starting with 1, this set starts with 0. One way to remember that is to think "whole - hole - a zero is like a hole."

$$\{0, 1, 2, 3, 4, 5, \ldots \}$$

Integers
The integers is a new set of numbers you are probably just beginning to work with. The set of integers is a set of positive and negative numbers. Some people describe the set of integers as the set of natural numbers and its opposites (negative numbers) and zero.

$$\{ \ldots, -3, -2, -1, 0, 1, 2, 3, \ldots \}$$

Numbers continued

Rational Numbers

Though you may not be familiar with the term rational number, you have been using rational numbers for many years. A rational number is simply a number that can be written as a fraction of integers. Some examples of rational numbers are ⅔ and ⁻⁵⁄₁₉.

2 is rational because it can be written as ²⁄₁.

3.5 is rational because it can be written as 3⁵⁄₁₀ or ³⁵⁄₁₀.

As you can see, just about every type of number you have ever seen can be called a rational number.

Irrational Numbers

These are obviously numbers that do not fit into the set of rational numbers. What numbers could be left that couldn't be written as a fraction of integers? There are a few numbers that have decimals that do not repeat any pattern. For example, the most famous irrational number is π. Mathematicians, even with the help of powerful computers, have been unable to find an end to the decimals of π. Most often, 3.14 or ²²⁄₇ is used for π, but these are only approximations.

Later on in this book, you will be introduced to square roots. Many square roots are also irrational because they have decimals that continue indefinitely with no set pattern.

Real Numbers

Every set of numbers talked about so far belongs to the set of real numbers. Even irrational numbers are real numbers. This is a term used to describe all numbers that can be written as decimals.

Imaginary Numbers

The only numbers that are not real are unreal, or imaginary. You will learn more about imaginary numbers if you take a class in advanced algebra.

As you can see, mathematics is very balanced. There is a name for every type of number. There's even a name for those numbers that fall outside a particular set. If there is such a thing as a googellybob, then there is probably also an un-googellybob. Mathematicians like to investigate both. Learning about un-googellybobs may teach you much about googellybobs.

Numbers Practice

Name _____

In each box below, circle the numbers that do not belong.

1. Natural Numbers

2	-57	⅖
0	12	
0.5	14	1,062

2. Whole Numbers

185	⅗	98
7	0	
1.6	-2	419

3. Integers

202	-157	¹⁵⁄₂₁
50	-12.75	
1	0	-2,517

4. Rational Numbers

2⅔	-16	-⁹⁄₇
4.215	π	
-1	0	65%

Test Your Knowledge

Without looking back, write your own definition of each of the following sets of numbers.

5. Whole Numbers _____
_____
_____

6. Integers _____
_____
_____

7. Rational Numbers _____
_____
_____

8. Irrational Numbers _____
_____

FS-10211 Pre-Algebra Step-by-Step

Numbers Practice continued

In the diagram below, each oval represents a set of numbers. Since the members of the set of natural numbers is a part of all of the other sets described on the previous pages except one, it is in the middle. The next oval out should contain a set of numbers that includes all the natural numbers and zero. Complete the diagram. Within each oval, write the name of the set it represents. Also write a few of its members that do not belong in the previous set.

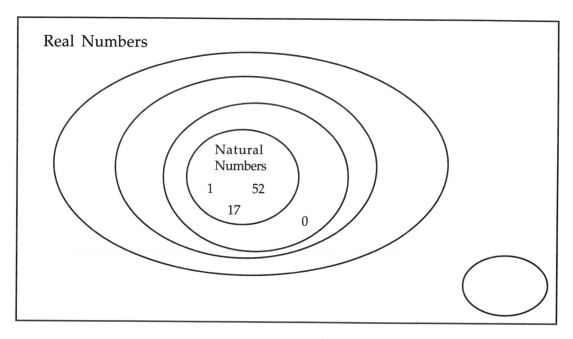

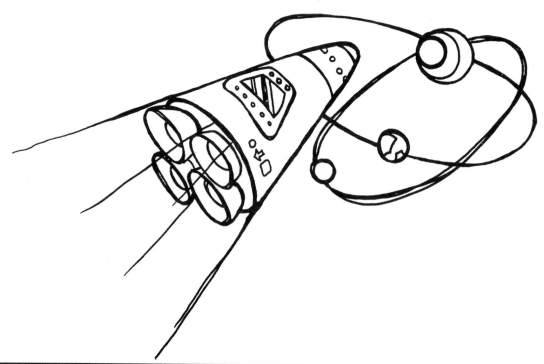

FS-10211 Pre-Algebra Step-by-Step

Properties

When working with numbers, it is helpful to know a few shortcut methods. The properties below and on pages 11-12 are exactly that, shortcuts. They teach a little about the character of numbers. These properties are true for all real numbers. They may be used at any time to juggle numbers to make them easier to work with. Each property is shown with an example of how it can be used as a shortcut.

The first property is one that is used almost every day and you probably don't even think about it.

Commutative Property	
$n + s = s + n$	$ns = sn$

This property says that it's ok to change the order of the numbers when adding or multiplying. This is very helpful when you are working with a long string of numbers. Sometimes it is easier to compute one pair of numbers in your head than another. Below are a couple examples that show how the commutative property makes mental math quite easy.

$75 + 312 + 25 =$
$75 + 25 + 312 =$
$100 + 312 = 412$

$17 \times 40 \times 5 =$
$40 \times 5 \times 17 =$
$200 \times 17 = 3,400$

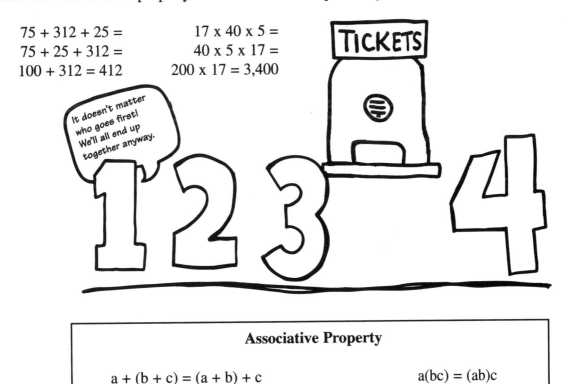

Associative Property	
$a + (b + c) = (a + b) + c$	$a(bc) = (ab)c$

This is another property that is used almost without thinking. It is very similar to the commutative property. Instead of changing the order of numbers, this property shows that it's ok to change how numbers are grouped (associated).

$(16 + 17) + 13 =$
$16 + (17 + 13) =$
$16 + 30 = 46$

$4 \times (25 \times 47) =$
$(4 \times 25) \times 47 =$
$100 \times 47 = 4,700$

Properties continued

Below are two properties that appear to be obvious. They probably weren't obvious to you in first grade, but they are now. The identity properties simply show you that taking a number and adding zero or multiplying by one doesn't change the number at all. In other words, the identity of the number is not changed.

Additive Identity Property
$n + 0 = n$

$257 + 356 - 257 = ?$

Remember the
commutative property?

$257 - 257 + 356 = ?$

Because of the
additive identity property,
solving the rest of this is a snap.

$0 + 356 = ?$
$0 + 356 = 356$

Multiplicative Identity Property
$1 \cdot n = n$

Does $\frac{2}{3}$ equal $\frac{10}{15}$?

$\frac{2}{3} \times \frac{5}{5} = \frac{10}{15}$
$\frac{5}{5} = 1$

Because of the
multiplicative identity property,

$\frac{2}{3}$ must equal $\frac{10}{15}$.

Closely related to the two identity properties are the two inverse properties. These properties show what can be done to "undo" addition and multiplication. In algebra, you will be doing a lot of "undoing" to solve problems.

Additive Inverse Property
$n + -n = 0$

Addition can be "undone" by means of subtraction or by adding the same number having the opposite sign.

$27 + 15 - 15 = 27$

Subtracting 15 is a way of "undoing" the adding of 15. The 27 is left unchanged.

Multiplicative Inverse Property
$n \cdot \frac{1}{n} = 1$

Multiplication can be "undone" by means of division or by multiplying by the reciprocal.*

$5 \times 7 \times \frac{1}{7} = 5$

Dividing by 7, or multiplying by $\frac{1}{7}$ is a way of "undoing" the multiplying by 7. The 5 is left unchanged.

---

*Remember how you divide fractions? $\frac{1}{2} \div 3 = \frac{1}{2} \times \frac{1}{3}$
Dividing by a number and multiplying by its reciprocal produce the same results.

Properties continued

Below is another property that is very easy to learn. It points out a unique quality of the number zero. No matter what you multiply by zero, the result is always zero.

> **Multiplication Property of Zero**
> $0 \cdot n = 0$

Just try to increase a
quantity with me around.
I will reduce your efforts
to nothing!

The final property below is helpful when working with long strings of numbers to compute that include parentheses. This property shows an alternate way to work with a number being multiplied by a sum or difference contained in parentheses.

> **Distributive Property**
> $a(b + c) = ab + ac$

Multiplication Over Addition
$4(25 + 10) = 4(25) + 4(10)$
$4(35) = 100 + 40$
$140 = 140$

Multiplication Over Subtraction
$5(52 - 22) = 5(52) - 5(22)$
$5(30) = 260 - 110$
$150 = 150$

Sometimes one method is easier than the other. Look carefully at the two examples above. If you were to solve those problems using mental math, which do you think would be the easiest way to calculate each answer? Write your answer and explanation on the lines below.

_____

_____

_____

_____

_____

Properties Practice

The properties discussed on pages 10-12 are very helpful when you have no paper and pencil or calculator. The properties provide ways of manipulating numbers so that they are easier to calculate mentally.

Use properties to solve the following problems mentally. For the first two problems, tell what property you use for each step.

<u>Steps</u>   <u>Properties</u>

1. $117 + 96 + 83 + 3(6 + 2) =$

    $117 + 96 + 83 + \underline{\hspace{1cm}} =$ _____

    $117 + 83 + 96 + \underline{\hspace{1cm}} =$ _____

    $\underline{\hspace{0.7cm}} + \underline{\hspace{0.7cm}} = \underline{\hspace{0.7cm}}$

2. $(22 + 57) + 28 - 57 =$

    $(22 + \underline{\hspace{1cm}}) + \underline{\hspace{1cm}} - \underline{\hspace{1cm}} =$ _____

    $\underline{\hspace{0.7cm}} + \underline{\hspace{0.7cm}} = \underline{\hspace{0.7cm}}$ _____

3. $57 \times 26 \times 0 \times 13 = \underline{\hspace{1cm}}$ _____

4. $x + 0 = \underline{\hspace{1cm}}$ _____

5. $4 \times 22 \times 25 = \underline{\hspace{1cm}}$ _____

6. $(22 \times 4) \times 25 = \underline{\hspace{1cm}}$ _____

7. $18 \times \frac{1}{18} + 370 = \underline{\hspace{1cm}}$ _____

8. $259(10 + 10) = \underline{\hspace{1cm}}$ _____

9. $y + x - x = \underline{\hspace{1cm}}$ _____

Algebraic Lingo

Every subject has its own jargon, or lingo. Jargon is simply words used exclusively in relation to one particular subject. Baseball jargon includes RBI, home run, stolen base, etc. Below are a few of the words you will encounter when studying algebra. Knowing what they mean will make learning algebra much easier. These aren't all the new words you will encounter, but they are ones you will see most often.

expression 36×14

An expression is a mathematical phrase or grouping of numbers. An expression does not have another value to which it is equal. $36 \times 14 = 504$ is not an expression.

equation $36 \times 14 = 504$

An equation is a statement that describes two equal values. These equal values are separated by an equal sign.

inequality $36 \times 14 \geq 500$

An inequality compares two values that may or may not be equal. It is very similar to an equation except that the equal sign is replaced by a sign of inequality such as $<, \leq, >, \geq,$ or $\neq$.

variable $x + 7 = 32$

The variable is the key to algebra. The x in the equation above is a variable. Anytime a letter is put in the place of a number, the letter is called a variable. While the x may represent a value of 25 in this equation, it may represent 259 in another equation. Its value varies, which is why it is called a variable.

constant $35 + s$

A constant is something that remains the same. In this expression, s is a variable because it can be changed; 35 is a constant.

coefficient $7y \qquad 7(x + 42)$

A coefficient is a constant that is being multiplied by a variable or by another expression. Seven is a coefficient in each of the two expressions above.

solution $n + 19 = 21 \qquad\qquad w + 7 < 10$
                                                   $n = 2 \qquad\qquad\qquad w \; \varepsilon \; \{2, 1, 0, \ldots\}$

A solution or solution set is a number or set of numbers that can replace a variable to produce a true equation or inequality. Two is the only number that can replace n in the equation above that will produce a true equation.

term $2r + 34s + 17 + 14r + 7rs = 47$

Terms are simply elements of an expression, equation, or inequality. In the expression above, 2r, 34s, 17, 14r, and 7rs are all terms. 2r and 14r are also called *like terms* since they are both made up of a constant and r. 7rs is not a like term in relation to 2r or 34s.

Algebraic Lingo Practice

Use your new algebraic lingo to complete the crossword puzzle below. Some of the words in the puzzle are ones you already know.

Across

1. a letter that represents a number
4. answer to an addition problem
5. answer to a multiplication problem
7. a single element in an expression, equation, or inequality
10. the number that can replace a variable in an equation to make it a true equation
11. the largest set of numbers that includes all the numbers you have ever used
12. ____ numbers are all numbers that can be written as fractions.
13. the set of numbers that includes the natural numbers, their opposites, and 0
14. $4n + 2 = 25$ is an example of an ____.
15. $2y + 9 = 17$, 2 can be called a(n) ____

Down

2. The ____ property shows that numbers can be regrouped when being added or multiplied without changing their value.
3. $5x + 2$ is an example of a(n) ____.
6. a number statement in which two values are compared
8. $a + b = b + a$ shows the ____ property.
9. A number that stands alone in an equation can be called a ____ .

Order of Operations

Drivers are given "rules of the road" that govern how they drive. These rules include stopping at red lights and at stop signs, yielding to on-coming traffic when making a left turn, etc.

In math, there are also "rules of the road." These rules govern the order in which numbers are computed. They are called the "order of operations." When you must solve a long string of computations, the order of operations tells you what should receive your attention first.

<u>The Order of Operations:</u>
Parentheses
Exponents
Multiplication and
Division
Addition and
Subtraction

Some people use a memory aid to remember the order of operations. Using the first initials of the words above, the following sentence was created:

Please **E**xcuse **My D**ear **A**unt **S**ally.

It may be easier to remember this sentence than to remember the order of operations. Using the initials of each of the words, you can recall the words they represent.

Order of Operations continued

Put the order of operations to use. Below is an example that includes every step in the order of operations. It shows how you can work through a long number sentence following the "rules of the road."

$$7^2 - (15 + 22) + 16 \div 2 \times 6 =$$

P - Parentheses

$$7^2 \quad - \quad 37 \quad + 16 \div 2 \times 6 =$$

E - Exponents

$$49 \quad - \quad 37 \quad + 16 \div 2 \times 6 =$$

M - Multiplication and
D - Division
(Solve from left to right.)

$$49 \quad - \quad 37 \quad + \quad 8 \quad \times 6 =$$

$$49 \quad - \quad 37 \quad + \quad 48 =$$

A - Addition and
S - Subtraction
(Solve from left to right.)

$$12 \quad + \quad 48 =$$

$$60$$

Without knowing about the order of operations, the previous problem could be solved differently and a different answer could be found. For example, if all the multiplication and exponents were done first, you would get the following number sentence:

$$49 - (15 + 22) + 16 \div 12$$

Then, solving from left to right, the following solution would be found:

$$49 - 37 + 16 \div 12 =$$
$$28 \div 12 =$$
$$2 \tfrac{1}{3}$$

As you can see, it is very important that everyone follow the same "rules of the road." Otherwise, one number sentence could have several different answers. Following the order of operations, there is only one possible solution.

FS-10211 Pre-Algebra Step-by-Step

Order of Operations Practice

Follow the order of operations to solve the number sentences below. Match each number sentence with its solution in the column on the right. Use the letters that correspond with each numbered problem to read the coded message.

_____ 1. $15 - (4 + 7)$

_____ 2. $5 \times 2^3 - (27 - 21)$

_____ 3. $8 + 6 \times 4 \div 8 - 5$

_____ 4. $3^3 \div (3 \times 3)$

_____ 5. $9 + 7 - 5 \times 3 + 10$

_____ 6. $32 \div 4 + 4 \times 3$

_____ 7. $3 + 4^3 - 7 \times 6$

_____ 8. $28 + (97 - 3^4) - 5 \times 7$

_____ 9. $90 \div 5 \times 2 + 16$

_____ 10. $5^3 - 84 \div 12 - (6 \times 3)$

_____ 11. $98 \div (15 - 8) \times 12$

_____ 12. $67 + 6^2 \times 6 \div (2 + 1)$

_____ 13. $114 - 16 \times 3 + 27 - 4$

_____ 14. $8^2 - (2 + 6 \times 4)$

A. 25
B. 2
C. 52
D. 4
E. 168
F. 19
G. 100
H. 9
I. 89
J. 18
K. 43
L. 11
M. 38
N. 139
O. 34
P. 360
Q. 317
R. 6
S. 20
T. 3
U. 36
V. 98
W. 10
X. 206
Y. 27
Z. 32

```
__ __ __ __  __ __ __ V  __ __ __  __ __ __  __ __ __ __
10  2  2  1   1  3 13    11  3  6    7 12  1   10  2  2  1

__ __ __ __ __ __ __ __ __ __ __ __ __  __ __ __ __ __ __
14  7  4  8 11 14  7  4 13  9 13  7 12  6  14  7  6  4 11  3

__ __ __  __ U __ __ __  __ F __ __ __  __ __ __ __ .
 4  8 11   3    5 11  6    2    4  8 11   3  2  7  1
```

One of the largest hurdles students must overcome in order to be successful in algebra is the understanding of integers. Working with integers seems to contradict everything students have learned about math. In this chapter, every attempt has been made to show students that the "rules" of integer computation make sense.

On the pages dealing with investigating integer addition and subtraction (pages 23 and 28), students are taught a game involving chips. This game should lead students to discover the rules for themselves. Discovering these rules on their own should help students better understand them.

Students seem to have less difficulty with multiplication and division of integers. The rules are easy to remember, yet they often do not make sense to the student. Real-world examples are given for all forms of computation with integers. Instead of simply being numbers on a page, the students will see integers come to life in the world around them. This should give students the additional support they need to get over the integer hurdle.

If this is the first time your students have seen integers, you may want to do a few more introductory activities. Posting a large number line on a wall in the classroom is helpful.

To help your students get in touch with integers in the real world, have them draw a picture of a situation in which integers can be used. They should also draw a number line to go with it. For example, students could draw a picture of an ocean scene with cliffs beside it. The number line could then be drawn vertically with zero at sea level, positive numbers above sea level, and negative numbers below sea level.

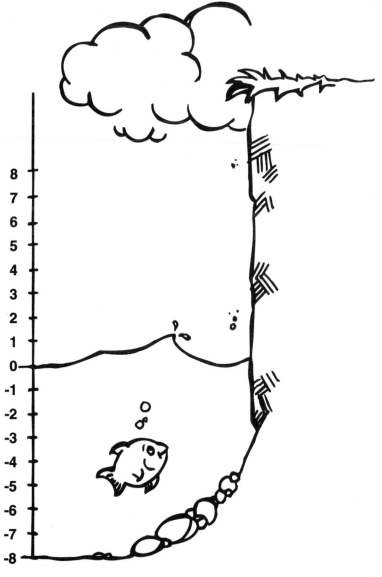

To provide students with additional practice with working with integers, the game discussed in the investigation sections (pages 23 and 28) can be extended. To extend the game, the following materials are needed: 20 chips each of two different colors, 40 white stickers, a cup. Place a sticker on each of the chips. On each sticker, write the numbers from 1 to 20. Make one set of chips (all of one color) positive and the other set negative. Put all the chips in a cup.

Organize students in pairs. One student will be negative, the other positive. Before the game starts, tell the student which operation to use (+, −, x, or ÷). The students can flip a coin to see who goes first.

To start a turn, each student draws one chip from the cup. They create a number sentence using the operation you chose. The first number drawn is the first one in the number sentence.

The students calculate the answer. If the answer is positive, the positive student wins the turn. If the answer is negative, the negative student wins the turn. The winner of the turn writes the answer on a slip of paper that will be his or her personal score card. The chips are put to the side.

Play continues in this fashion with students alternating drawing the first chip until all the chips have been used. At the end of the game, the students add up all the numbers on their own score card. The student whose total has the greatest absolute value is the winner of the game.

If you want students to have mixed practice with integers, the game may be changed slightly. Allow the person who drew the second chip to declare the operation to be used. This will allow students to develop a strategy for their game. Depending on the numbers, a student could choose the operation that will allow him or her to win that particular turn.

What Are Integers?

In the previous chapter, you learned that the set of integers consists of the natural numbers, their opposites, and zero.

$$\{ \ldots, -3, -2, -1, 0, 1, 2, 3 \ldots \}$$

On the number line, the set of integers looks like this:

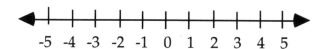

You have probably never thought of numbers having opposites. The opposite of any number can be found on the number line. A number's opposite lies the same distance from zero on the opposite side of zero. So, the opposite of 3 is -3. 3 and -3 both lie three units away from zero, one on its right side and the other on its left. The opposite of -3 is 3.

Adding Integers

When you first learned to add, you may have used a number line. To add 3 and 2, you found that you could start on the 3 and jump two units to the right and land on 5. You can use the number line to add integers, too. The only difference is that when you see a negative number, you move in the opposite direction as you would if the number were positive. For example, to add -3 and -2, you start on -3. When you add positive numbers, you always move to the right. But since you are adding a negative number, you move to the left.

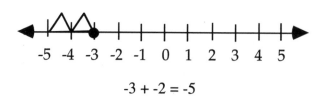

$$-3 + -2 = -5$$

What Are Integers? continued

The same can be done if only one of the numbers is negative.

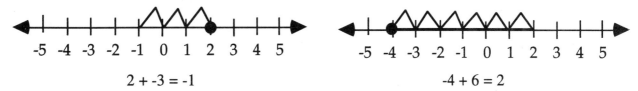

$$2 + -3 = -1$$

$$-4 + 6 = 2$$

Look carefully at the example above on the right. Why should you move to the right instead of the left? In this case, because you are adding a positive number to a negative number, you move to the right. When the number you are adding is positive, you move to the right.

But how does this work in the real world? When are negative numbers used? One area in which negative numbers come up a great deal is money. The financial account of the U.S. government has a negative balance. The government is several billion dollars in debt. Whenever you owe someone money, you are in debt. Your debt can be described as a negative number. Below are two examples of how negative numbers are used.

Example A: You have borrowed $25 from your mom. (Since this is an amount you owe, it can be described as -25.) After earning some money from baby-sitting, you pay your mom $12. (This is your payback amount. It is positive.) How much do you still owe your mom? This can be answered by solving the following equation:

$$-25 + 12 = -13$$

You still owe your mom $13.

Example B: After paying your mom $12 of what you owe her, you find you need to borrow an additional $30. For how much are you now in debt?

$$-13 + -30 = -43$$

You are now $43 in debt to your mom.

Name _____

Investigating Integer Addition

You can explore addition of integers with an exciting game. In this game, you will use chips to mirror what happens when integers are added. In order to play, you will need 20 chips, each of two different colors. The game is described using red and blue chips, but you can use chips of any color. If you do not have chips, you can use other small objects. You may use colored paper as a last resort.

If the chips, or other objects, can be written on, draw plus signs (+) on one set and negative signs, or minus signs (-), on the other. In the descriptions below, the red chips are negative, and the blue chips are positive.

Even though they are opposites, these red and blue chips are quite friendly. They like to pair up any chance they get. Just like the saying goes, opposites attract. Below is a drawing that shows what happens when a group of 7 blue (+) chips meets up with 3 red (-) chips.

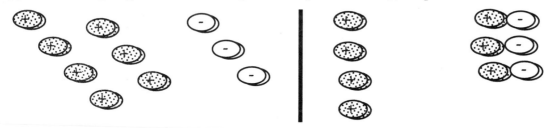

The funny thing is that every time blue and red chips meet, they pair up, and the pairs vanish in a flash leaving behind any remaining chips.

These chips act in the same manner as integers. The example above shows exactly what happens when you add 7 and -3. The opposites pair up and vanish leaving positive 4.

Use your chips to determine the results of the following situations. Describe what chips are left. The remaining chips should be all red (-) or all blue (+) since all the pairs vanish. Keep all ten groupings of your chips for the activity on page 24.

1. -5 + 3 = _____

2. 8 + -6 = _____

3. -4 + -8 = _____

4. 4 + 3 = _____

5. 10 + -5 = _____

6. -10 + 5 = _____

7. -2 + -3 = _____

8. 6 + -6 = _____

9. 5 + 7 = _____

10. -10 + 10 = _____

Name _____

Addition Investigation Follow-Up

Once an investigator has collected sufficient data, he or she carefully analyzes the data and draws conclusions. You created data on page 23. You determined the results of ten different pairings of chips. Sort the ten pairings into the different cases listed below. Look carefully at the results for each type of pairing. Look for a pattern. If needed, calculate the results of several more pairings to test your theory. Then write a conclusion. What happens every time these pairings are made?

1. Case I - A group of positive chips meets another group of positive chips.

   _____
   _____
   _____

2. Case II - A group of negative chips meets another group of negative chips.

   _____
   _____
   _____

3. Case III - A group of negative chips meets a group of positive chips.
   A - There are more negative chips than positive chips.

   _____
   _____
   _____

4. Case III - A group of negative chips meets a group of positive chips.
   B - There are more positive chips than negative chips.

   _____
   _____
   _____

5. Case IV - Equal numbers of positive and negative chips meet.

   _____
   _____
   _____

6. How will understanding these four cases help when adding integers?

   _____
   _____
   _____

Name _____

Adding in Real-Life Situations

The problems below give more examples of how integers are used outside the math classroom. For the first few problems, the expression to be solved is given. Use what you learned with the chips to solve the problems. For the second half of the questions, you will write the expression to be solved. Look back at the first questions for assistance.

1. Sara borrowed $50 from her Dad. After earning money with a part-time job, Sara paid her Dad $23. How much money does Sara still owe her Dad?

   $-50 + 23 =$ _____

2. In the afternoon, Julio heard part of a weather report. The meteorologist said the temperature had risen 25° from the early morning temperature of -15°F. What was the afternoon temperature?

   $-15 + 25 =$ _____

3. The Jets started a play on their 35 yard line but were pushed back 10 yards. On what yard line are they now?

   $35 + -10 =$ _____

4. A submarine is in the ocean 3,000 ft below sea level. The captain has given orders to bring the sub up 1,200 ft. How far below sea level will this change put them?

   $-3,000 + 1,200 =$ _____

5. Ken borrowed $250 from a bank and $125 from a friend. By how much is Ken in debt?

   _____

6. At 5:00 a.m., the temperature was -5°C. By noon, the temperature had risen 11°. What was the temperature at noon?

   _____

7. The opening stock price for Pizza Pete's was 56. During the day, the price fell 7 points. What was the stock's selling price at closing?

   _____

8. Karen had a balance of $57 in her checking account. She wrote a check for $90. What is her new balance?

   _____

Subtracting Integers

The nice thing about subtracting integers is that a subtraction problem can easily be changed to an addition problem. When solving the problems on page 25, your first thought in some cases may have been to subtract. The subtraction sign (-) and the negative sign (-) are exactly the same sign and are easily interchanged. In other words, the two problems shown on the number lines below are exactly the same. As you can see, their results are the same.

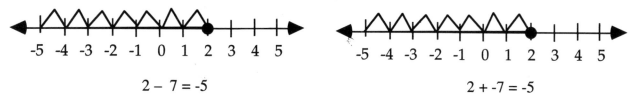

$$2 - 7 = -5 \qquad\qquad 2 + -7 = -5$$

Both the subtraction sign and the negative sign on a number tell you to move in the opposite direction, or negative direction, on the number line. Here's another example to help you see how this works:

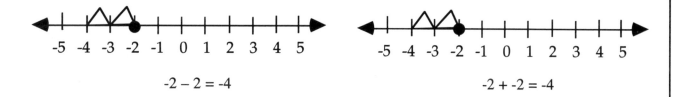

$$-2 - 2 = -4 \qquad\qquad -2 + -2 = -4$$

There's one curiosity that shows up when you subtract a negative number. Remember: A negative sign tells you to do the opposite. So when two negative signs are together, you have to do the opposite of what you would normally do when you see one negative sign. What is the opposite action? Addition.

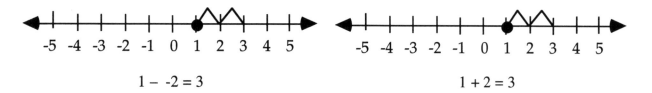

$$1 - -2 = 3 \qquad\qquad 1 + 2 = 3$$

You may understand this better by considering what it means when two negatives are used in a row in the English language. Imagine that you have two friends who are not the same nationality as you. Another person you thought was a friend says that you should not spend time with these people because they are "different." Their difference makes them not as good as you. You can't believe you are hearing this. You tell this so-called friend, "I'm not going to avoid my friends because they are different." What do you mean by this? "Avoid" is a word with a negative connotation. "Not" is also a negative word. These two negative words cancel each other out. What you are saying in this sentence is ultimately positive. You WILL spend time with your friends.

Subtracting Integers continued

Read the problems below to see how subtracting integers plays a role in everyday situations.

At 10:00 p.m., the temperature is -2°C. By 6:00 a.m., the temperature has dropped 7 degrees. What is the temperature at 6:00 a.m.?

$$-2 - 7 = -2 + -7 = -9$$

The temperature is -9°C.

John has borrowed $350 to pay some bills. He decides to call the bank to check the balance in his checking account to find out how much more he needs to save in order to pay back the loan. He finds his balance is $47. How much more does John need to save to pay back the loan?

$$350 - 47 = 350 + -47 = 303$$

John must save $303.

Look at the example above again. What if John found out he had bounced a few checks so that his balance was -$62. Now how much must he save?

$$350 - -62 = 350 + 62 = 412$$

John must save $412. He has to save $350 to pay off the loan and another $62 to bring his checking account balance back to zero. So it makes sense that these two amounts should be added.

Investigating Integer Subtraction

Continue the game that was started with addition. You will need to know a little bit more about the character of these chips. Sometimes a group of chips sets out in search of more of their same kind. Many times, they need a certain number of their own kind to go see a movie with a group of the opposite kind. They call this being "on the take." When chips are on the take, they take as many of their own kind as they already have. So, if 5 blue (+) chips are on the take, they are in search of 5 blue (+) chips.

A funny thing happens when there is not enough of one group to satisfy the take. The group on the take demands that the other group find enough pairs of chips to satisfy its take.

Seven blue (+) chips meet up with three red (-) chips on the take. The red (-) chips demand three red (-) chips.

One blue (+) chip scout goes out and finds 3 pairs of chips and brings them back to the group.

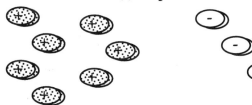
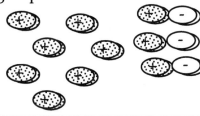

The red (-) chips take the 3 red (-) chips and leave the blue (+) chips alone.

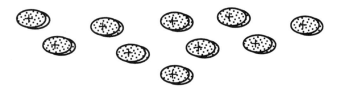

Use your chips to determine the result of the situations below. The group on the take is the group described after the subtraction sign.

1. 5 – 3 = _____

2. -7 – -5 = _____

3. 2 – 5 = _____

4. -4 – -6 = _____

5. -6 – 3 = _____

6. 4 – -1 = _____

7. 2 – -5 = _____

8. -8 – 3 = _____

9. -10 – 6 = _____

10. 6 – 14 = _____

Subtraction Investigation Follow-Up

What did you discover during this investigation? Describe your findings on the lines below.

1. Case I - Two groups of chips with the same sign meet.
   A. The group on the take is smaller than the group it meets.

   _____

   _____

2. Case I - Two groups of chips with the same sign meet.
   B. The group on the take is larger than the group it meets.

   _____

   _____

3. Case II - Two groups of chips with opposite signs meet.
   A. The negative chips are on the take.

   _____

   _____

4. Case II - Two groups of chips with opposite signs meet.
   A. The positive chips are on the take.

   _____

   _____

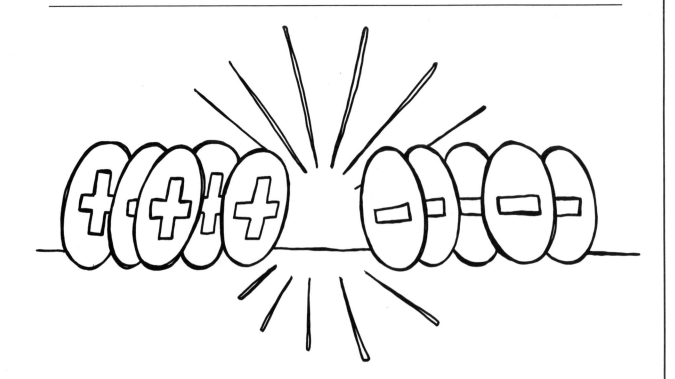

Subtracting in Real-Life Situations

The problems below give more examples of how integers are used outside the math classroom. For the first few problems, the expression to be solved is given. Use what you learned with the chips to solve the problems. For the second half of the questions, you will write the expression to be solved. Look back at the first questions for assistance.

1. The temperature at noon was -1°C. A storm blew in causing the temperature to drop 8 degrees by 4:00 p.m. What was the temperature at 4:00 p.m.?

   -1 – 8 = _____

2. A submarine is 500 yards below sea level when it dives 100 yards further below sea level. Find its current location.

   -500 – 100 = _____

3. Karen borrowed $75 from her parents. She paid back $37. How much does she still owe?

   75 – 37 = _____

4. Rita had $117 in her checking account before she wrote a check for $123. What is her new balance?

   117 – 123 = _____

5. The bank charged Rita a fee of $25 for bouncing a check. What will her balance be when the fee is charged to her account?

   _____

6. Christopher went mountain climbing. He climbed 4,120 feet above sea level before finding a place to camp for the night. The next day, he descended 1,375 feet. Find his current location.

   _____

7. An elevator picked up passengers on the 5th floor and descended 7 floors before letting them off. On what floor did the passengers exit the elevator?

   _____

8. The temperature at 5:00 p.m. was 5°C. The temperature dropped 9 degrees by midnight. What was the temperature at midnight?

   _____

Multiplying and Dividing Integers

The multiplication and division of integers is no different than the multiplication and division of whole numbers. Just one more step is added and that is determining the sign on the answer. Below and on page 32 are a couple of real-life examples.

As a special gift to her seven grandchildren, Mrs. Forrest gave each of them a check for $25. How will Mrs. Forrest's checking account be affected?

The action of spending money is negative. The grandchildren are positive. To solve this problem, you can solve the following equation:

$$-25 \times 7 = ?$$

Multiply as you normally would if both numbers were positive. $25 \times 7 = 175$
The question is, what is the sign on the answer? Is it negative or positive? Is the effect on Mrs. Forrest's checking account positive or negative? Since her balance will decrease because of money leaving her account, the answer is -$175.

During a scientific experiment, Crystal recorded the temperature of a substance every 5 minutes. Each time, she noticed the temperature decreased by exactly 3°. Crystal took the substance's temperature 10 times. By how much did the temperature change over the course of the experiment?

$$-3 \times 10 = ?$$

Multiplying the 3 and the 10 gives you 30. Should 30 be positive or negative? Did the temperature change in a negative or positive direction? Decreasing temperature is a negative action. So the answer is -30°.

Multiplying and Dividing Integers continued

Four friends worked together to organize a dance party. They paid for the music and refreshments and charged an admission fee to recover some of the costs. They agreed to equally share in any debt or income that could result. After the party, they met to settle the costs. They found that they were short in paying the bills by $48. How did this affect each friend's savings?

$$-48 \div 4 = ?$$

Divide 48 by 4 as you normally would. The answer is 12. Is the 12 positive or negative? Will the friend's savings increase or decrease? Since each friend has to help cover the debt, their savings will decrease by $12. The answer is -$12.

Ted can rappel down the side of a mountain at a rate of 70 ft/minute. How long should it take him to rappel a 1,400 ft cliff?

$$-1,400 \div -70 = ?$$

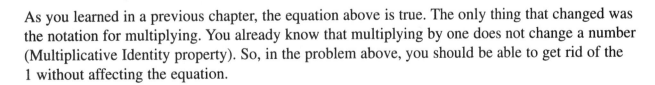

Dividing 1,400 by 70 gives a quotient of 20. Should the answer be positive or negative? The answer represents the amount of time it takes Ted to rappel a cliff. Is this time positive or negative? A negative time represents going back in time, a reverse direction. So the answer to this problem is positive 20.

Assigning a sign to the answer to such problems relates to the patterns you found when subtracting negative numbers— two negatives become positive.

$$-1 \ x \ -5 = -1(-5)$$

As you learned in a previous chapter, the equation above is true. The only thing that changed was the notation for multiplying. You already know that multiplying by one does not change a number (Multiplicative Identity property). So, in the problem above, you should be able to get rid of the 1 without affecting the equation.

$$-1(-5) = -(-5)$$

When you find two negatives in a subtraction problem, like 4 − -5, what do you do? You add. The two negatives change to a positive. The same is true here.

$$-(-5) = 5$$

Making Sense of Integer Multiplication and Division

After reading pages 31 and 32, answer the questions below.

1. Considering the examples given, what sign do you think the answer should be to a problem in which a negative number is multiplied by a positive number?

   _____

   _____

2. Considering the examples given, what sign do you think the answer should be to a problem in which a negative number is divided by a positive number?

   _____

   _____

3. How is multiplication related to division? Can a division problem be rewritten as an equivalent multiplication problem?

   _____

   _____

   _____

4. What sign do you think the answer should be to a problem in which two negative numbers are either multiplied or divided?

   _____

   _____

5. Describe one way you can help yourself remember what sign to place on the answer of a multiplication or division problem involving integers.

   _____

   _____

   _____

Solve.

6. $-6 \times 4 =$ _____

7. $-84 \div 4 =$ _____

8. $-49 \div -7 =$ _____

9. $-15 \times -3 =$ _____

10. $6 \times -21 =$ _____

11. $55 \div -5 =$ _____

FS-10211 Pre-Algebra Step-by-Step

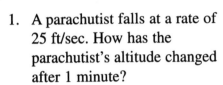

Multiplying and Dividing in Real-Life Situations

Solve each of the following problems using multiplication or division. Write an equation for problems 3-8.

1. A parachutist falls at a rate of 25 ft/sec. How has the parachutist's altitude changed after 1 minute?

    $-25 \times 60 = $ _____

2. Susan purchased her friend's 10-speed bike for $144. She has agreed to pay her friend in equal payments over the course of two months. If Susan pays a portion each week, how will her checking account be affected each week?

    $-144 \div 8 = $ ____

3. Paul purchased a stereo on layaway. His payments are $37 a month. Paul has written checks for 7 payments. How has this affected his checking account?

    _____

4. During a summer morning, the temperature increased 3° each hour from 6:00 a.m. until noon. What was the total change in temperature during these morning hours?

    _____

5. Jill can rappel a mountainside at a rate of 75 ft/min. How long should it take Jill to rappel a 1,725 ft cliff?

    _____

6. During four football plays, the Jets lost 24 yards. The coach noticed that they lost the same number of yards during each play. By how many yards did the Jet's position on the field change each play?

    _____

7. A group of six friends agreed to share the debts or profits from a dance party it planned. In the end, each friend paid $16. What was the financial result of the dance party?

    _____

8. In a large office building, one of the elevators is not working properly. No matter what floor you select to get off on, the elevator stops every two floors. If you want to go down eight floors, how many times will the elevator stop on its way (including the floor where you exit the elevator)?

    _____

3 —Basic Operations With Real Numbers-
Teaching Notes

This chapter gives students an opportunity to work with positive and negative decimals and fractions. Before starting this chapter, students may need a review of decimal and fraction computations. No instruction involving computational algorithms is given. Students are simply shown how to use what they learned from last chapter in relation to decimals and fractions.

If students have not yet mastered integer computation in the previous chapter, this chapter may supply the review and reinforcement they need. But if students have not mastered decimal and fraction computation, this is not the place to start. The material covered will only cause more frustration. It would be better for such students to skip this chapter entirely or embark on a review of decimal and fraction computation before returning to this chapter. Students will have no trouble going on without this chapter. There may be a few decimal and fraction computations in future chapters, but they will not be the majority.

Practice
To reinforce what is learned in this chapter, you may consider revising the game described in the teaching notes of Chapter 2. A new set of chips should be made with random decimals and fractions. In order for the game to be fair, the positive and negative chips should have the same decimals or fractions just with opposite signs.

Extension
One project involving negative real numbers used in the real world, namely, the stock market, closes this chapter. There are numerous other areas in which negative real numbers are used. As an additional project, you may have your students name one other topic or career in which negative real numbers are used. Have the students describe how these numbers are used. Ask each student to report his or her findings to the class. You may have the student create one word problem involving his or her topic. This problem can be presented to the class to solve.

How to Solve Problems With Decimals

Problems involving both negative and positive decimals or negative and positive fractions are solved using the same methods used when solving problems with integers, as described in the previous chapter. Pages 37-43 include examples of such problems. Some of them involve working through more than one step. Read through the examples below carefully. Then try the practice problems on page 37.

During an experiment, Yvonne weighed a beaker full of a certain substance every minute. Each time, she noticed the weight decreased by 3.75 mg. If the beaker held 800 mg of substance at the start of the experiment, how much should the contents weigh after 15 minutes?

First, find out by how much the weight has changed.

$$-3.75 \times 15 = -56.25$$

Next, determine the new weight of the substance.

$$800 + -56.25 = 743.75$$

The substance should weigh 743.75 mg after 15 minutes.

In another experiment, Yvonne mixed 10 mL of one substance with 15 mL of another substance and left them for a period of time. After removing the solid particles that formed, Yvonne found the amount of liquid had been reduced by 5.6 mL. How much of the mixture remained?

$$10 + 15 + -5.6 = 19.4$$

There remained 19.4 mL of liquid.

Solving Problems With Decimals

For each problem, write an expression and solve.

1. Before going to bed, Maria's temperature was 103.2°. Her fever broke in the night so that her morning temperature was 3.7 degrees lower. What was Maria's temperature the next morning?

   _____

2. Bernie's math average was 98.7. His recent test brought his average down 3.8 points. What's Bernie's current average?

   _____

3. Ned borrowed $500 from the bank and $200 from a friend. The balance in his savings account is $147.86. How much more will Ned have to save in order to pay back the two loans?

   _____

4. Pattie wrote checks for $45.52, $66.12, and $17.85 to pay certain bills. Before writing the checks, her checking account had a balance of $115.22. What will her balance be after the checks go through her account?

   _____

5. When Ken hang-glides, he reduces his altitude by 27.6 ft every minute. How long will it take Ken to glide down from a 648.6 ft cliff?

   _____

6. How much does Ken's altitude change in 30 minutes?

   _____

7. Gerry had a coupon for $0.25 off a frozen pizza. The grocery store has a special triple coupon deal and allows customers to use a single coupon on up to five items. By how much would his total grocery bill change if Gerry used the coupon to buy five frozen pizzas?

   _____

8. Karyn has a gift certificate worth $20 at Bob's Books. She has chosen four books that each cost $3.95. After purchasing these books and deducting the total from the certificate, how much would the certificate be worth?

   _____

How to Solve Problems With Fractions

For problems involving fractions, you must combine what you know about fractions with what you know about integers. Below are a few examples to get you started.

The stock for Greg's Gardening Supplies sold for 48 ⅛ on Monday morning. By the close of the stock market on Friday, the stock had fallen 1 ⅜. What was the selling price of the stock when the market closed on Friday?

$$48 \tfrac{1}{8} \ + \ {-1} \tfrac{3}{8} =$$
$$47 \tfrac{9}{8} \ + \ {-1} \tfrac{3}{8} = \ 46 \tfrac{6}{8} = \ 46 \tfrac{3}{4}$$

The selling price of stock for Greg's Gardening Supplies was 46 ¾ at market close on Friday.

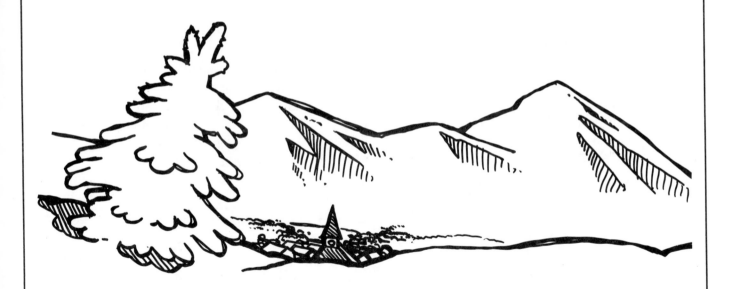

Each day for a week in a mountain town, ⅕ of a foot of snow melted, and ⅓ of a foot of additional snow fell. How much did the total accumulation of snow on the ground change in seven days?

$$(7) \ {-\tfrac{1}{5}} + \ (7) \ \tfrac{1}{3} =$$
$${-\tfrac{7}{5}} + \tfrac{7}{3} =$$
$${-\tfrac{21}{15}} + \tfrac{35}{15} = \tfrac{14}{15}$$

During that week, the accumulation of snow increased by ¹⁴⁄₁₅ of a foot.

Solving Problems With Fractions

For each problem, write an expression and solve.

1. Ben owns stock in an ice cream company. During the past week, prices fell 3 ⅞ points from a price of 26 ⅝. What is the current price of the stock?

_____

2. Albright Manufacturers purchased 1,000 lb of steel when they still had 236 ¼ lb left from their previous purchase. One project requires 1,200 lb of steel. When this project is completed, how much steel should be left over?

_____

3. During a month (30 days) in Caribou, Maine, it snowed every other day. The snow accumulated about ⅔ of a foot each time it snowed. On the days it didn't snow, the snow on the ground reduced by ⅖ of a foot. How much did the depth of snow change during that month?

_____

4. Harriet enjoys making her own bread. She bought a large sack of flour containing 100 cups. This past week, she has used the following amounts of flour in different recipes: 6 ½ cups, 4 ⅔ cups, 2 ¼ cups, 8 cups, and 4 ¾ cups. How much flour should be remaining in the sack?

_____

5. Irongate stock prices made the following changes over the course of a week: up 2 ⅛, down ⅜, down ½, up ⅛, and down 1 ¾. What was the overall change in the stock price for the week?

_____

6. Morgan is on a hike in the mountains. She can descend the mountain at a rate of 107 ½ ft/min. How long will it take her to descend a distance of 2,752 ft?

_____

The Stock Market

The project on pages 41-43 gives you the opportunity to use real numbers in a real-life situation. The stock market uses negative numbers to indicate that stock prices have gone down. Knowing how to work with negative numbers is necessary in understanding the stocks.

Stock prices fluctuate daily. In the financial section of a newspaper, you will find stock market prices for several major companies. The stock quotations found in the newspaper report valuable information for each stock that changes each day. Below is an example of a stock quote you may find in your local paper.

High	Low	Stock	Div.	Yld. %	P-E Ratio	Volume 100s	High	Low	Close	Net Change
$38\frac{3}{8}$	20	NYL	.30	.9	10	52	35	$34\frac{5}{8}$	$34\frac{7}{8}$	$-\frac{3}{8}$

The comments below describe what data is to be found in each column of the stock quote. First you will need to understand a few words used frequently when dealing with the stock market (*share*—units in which stock is sold; *stockholder or investor*—one who purchases stock; *investment*—amount of money paid for shares of stock; *dividend*—annual rate of interest earned on an investment).

High—the highest price per share at which this stock was traded during the past 52 weeks, current year-to-date

Low—the lowest price per share at which this stock was traded during the past 52 weeks, current year-to-date

Stock—the name of the company selling the stock and/or its three letter abbreviation

Div.—annual dividend per share a stockholder receives

Yld. %—the annual dividend an investor receives based on the closing price of the stock calculated using the formula Div. ÷ Close

P-E Ratio—an amount times the annual earnings the stock is currently selling at calculated by the formula Close ÷ Annual earnings per share (The annual earnings is not shown in the stock quote.)

Volume 100s—number of shares, in hundreds, traded that day

High—highest price per share the stock was traded for that day

Low—lowest price per share the stock was traded for that day

Close—price of the last trade of the day

Net Change—The difference between yesterday's and today's closing prices; Using the net change, you can calculate yesterday's closing price.

$$\text{Close} - \text{Net Change} = \text{Yesterday's Close}$$
$$34\tfrac{7}{8} - {}^{-}\tfrac{3}{8} = 35\tfrac{1}{4}$$

Following the Stock Market

Find the daily stock quotes in your local newspaper. Select five companies to watch during the next two to four weeks. These companies may sell your favorite game or food, or they could simply be five companies chosen at random. Use page 43 to chart their daily quotes. (Note: You will need five copies of page 43—one for each stock.) On the first and final days of recording, note the first and final year-to-date highs and lows and the dividend amount for each company in the table below.

Company	High		Low		Div.	
	First	Final	First	Final	First	Final

Immediately following the two to four week data collection, do the following using the data from each company:

1. Calculate the total change and the average daily change of the closing price.

2. Make line graphs for each company showing its daily closing prices.

3. Note on the graphs where year-to-date highs and lows changed, if at all.

4. Calculate the stock's average price and indicate this price on the graph.

Use your data and graph to answer the questions below and on page 42.

5. Imagine you are an investor. Choose one stock from the five you've tracked and calculate the following:

   A. Purchase 500 shares of stock at the low price on the first day you collected data. Calculate the total cost.   _____

   B. What percent of the stock sold that day did you purchase?   _____

   C. In a year's time, how much money will you earn in dividends?   _____

Following the Stock Market continued

5. D. Sell 250 shares of stock at the high price on the last day you collected data. Calculate the amount of money you will receive.

     _____

   E. What affect did your investment have on your savings?

     _____

6. Which stock had the greatest number of sales?

     _____

7. If you had purchased 500 shares of each stock at the low price on the first day you collected data, and sold them for the high price on the last day you collected data, which investment would have given you the greatest return? Which would have given you the least return?

_____

_____

8. Calculate the annual earnings per share for each company based on the final closing price. Follow the example below to help you.

Using the P-E Ratio, you can calculate the annual earnings per share. The P-E Ratio is found using the following formula:

$$\text{P-E Ratio} = \frac{\text{Close}}{\text{Annual earnings per share}}$$

For each company, you know the P-E Ratio and the closing price for each day. Writing the P-E Ratio over one, you have two equal fractions. The example below shows one way to calculate the annual earnings per share.

$$\frac{10}{1} = \frac{34\,\tfrac{7}{8}}{\text{Annual earnings per share}}$$

$$1 \times 34\,\tfrac{7}{8} = 10 \times \text{Annual earnings per share}$$

$$34\,\tfrac{7}{8} = 10 \times \text{Annual earnings per share}$$

(Note: $80 = 10 \times 8$ and $80 \div 10 = 8$ Any multiplication problem can be rewritten as a division problem.)

$$34\,\tfrac{7}{8} \div 10 = \text{Annual earnings per share}$$

$$3\,\tfrac{39}{80} \text{ or } 3.4875 = \text{Annual earnings per share}$$

If you own stock for a company with a P-E Ratio of 10 and a current closing price of $34\,\tfrac{7}{8}$ per share, you are earning about $3.49 per share on your investment.

Following the Stock Market continued

Company _____

Date	Yld. %	P-E Ratio	Sales 100s	High	Low	Close	Net change

Exponents and Roots
Teaching Notes

Students will probably be familiar with some of the topics covered in this chapter, such as exponents in general and scientific notation. But the material that follows gives students a little more depth in these areas. The connection between exponents and roots is highlighted and practical uses of both are shown.

This chapter would be appropriate to use after introducing students to exponents. Average to above-average students should be able to complete the material on their own. But, for more solid understanding, this chapter can be completed by a cooperative group of students. A heterogeneous group will work best.

To be successful in simplifying roots, students may need to review factors. Students may also need to spend more time on perfect roots. For groups that are having difficulties with this, suggest that they create a chart of perfect squares and cubes. This will help them discover factors that will simplify roots.

Pythagoras at Work
As a group project, have students plan an activity using the Pythagorean theorem. This project could be writing up the plans for a ramp to one of the entrances of the school or planning a large wall mural of geometric designs. Anything in relation to right angles that involves the students in measuring would be appropriate. If one group is less creative, its members may want to research the history of the Pythagorean theorem. They will find that this theorem was not discovered by Pythagoras. It was known in other parts of the world long before Pythagoras.

When the group projects are completed, have each group present its topic to the class. As part of its presentation, the group should have the class do at least one calculation involving the Pythagorean theorem that its members had to solve while completing the project.

Pythagoras Revisited
After students are instructed in solving algebraic equations, the Pythagorean theorem can be reconsidered in a new light. This theorem will be considered again in Chapter 5. Students will be able to calculate the length of one of the legs of a right triangle when they know the length of one leg and the hypotenuse.

Keep the students' work from this chapter as well as from their projects. Let the students review their work when they revisit Pythagoras in Chapter 5. The students will be able to double check their calculations using their new knowledge. You may even consider having them return to their groups and plan a new project covering all uses of the Pythagorean theorem (finding the length of the hypotenuse and finding the length of one leg).

Exponents

Name _____

Exponents can be very helpful when multiplying the same factor many times. Exponents are simply a shorthand notation for this multiplication, as in the example below.

$$2^8 = 2 \times 2 \times 2 \times 2 \times 2 \times 2 \times 2 \times 2 = 256$$

The exponent (8) tells how many of the base (2) needs to be multiplied.

Use what you know about exponents to fill in the blanks below.

1. ____^{4} = 5 x 5 x 5 x 5

2. 3^3 = ____ x ____ x ____

3. 2____ = 2 x 2 x 2 x 2 x 2 x 2

4. 7____ = 7

5. 2____ = 32

6. 5^5 = ____

Exponents can be any real number. The examples above showed all exponents to be natural numbers. What happens when the exponent is zero or a negative number? Look at the pattern below. Continue the pattern in order to answer the question yourself.

$2^4 = 16$
$2^3 = 2^4 \div 2 = 8$
$2^2 = 2^3 \div 2 = 4$

7. $2^1 =$ ___ $\div 2 = 2$

8. ___ $= 2^1 \div 2 =$ ___
$2^{-1} = 2^0 \div 2 = 2^0 \times \frac{1}{2} = \frac{1}{2} = \frac{1}{2^1}$

9. $2^{-2} =$ ___ $\div 2 =$ ___ $\times \frac{1}{2} =$ ___ $= \frac{1}{\_}$

10. $2^{-3} =$ _____

As you can see by the pattern, as the exponent gets smaller, the denominator of the fraction gets larger. Describe the pattern by completing the sentence below.

11. When any base has a negative exponent, it is equal to a fraction:

1 over _____

_____

Patterns of Powers

When you look carefully at a specific base raised to powers, you can usually find a pattern. The pattern that emerges with powers of ten is the easiest to recognize, and also, the most helpful. Fill in the blanks below to continue the pattern.

$$10^5 = 100,000$$
$$10^4 = 10,000$$

1. $10^3 = $ _____

2. $10^2 = $ _____

3. $10^1 = $ _____

4. $10^0 = $ _____

$$10^{-1} = 0.1$$
$$10^{-2} = 0.01$$

5. $10^{-3} = $ _____

6. $10^{-4} = $ _____

7. $10^{-5} = $ _____

8. What do you notice about the relationship between the number of zeros in the answer and the positive exponent on the base? How does the exponent being negative change the relationship?

_____

_____

_____

9. What do you notice about the movement of the decimal point. How does the sign on the exponent affect this?

_____

_____

_____

10. Do you think you would find the same patterns if you changed the base? Are these patterns true only for powers of ten? Explain your answer.

_____

_____

_____

Scientific Notation

One of the many practical uses for exponents and powers of ten is scientific notation. Scientists often work with very large numbers and very small numbers. Scientific notation makes it easier for scientists to record such data.

Below are a few examples of numbers written in scientific notation:

Distance from the Earth to the sun—9.296×10^7 miles
Speed of light through air—2.99×10^8 meters/second
Diameter of a hydrogen atom—1.06×10^{-9} meters
Mass of an electron—9.0×10^{-19} mg

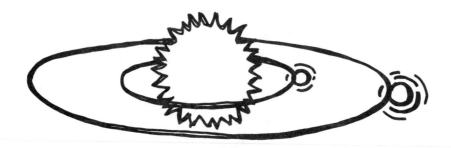

When you investigated the patterns of the powers of ten, you found that the only thing that changed was the placement of the decimal point. When the exponent is positive, the decimal point moves to the right making the number larger. When the exponent is negative, the decimal point moves to the left making the number smaller. The exponent also tells the number of places to move the decimal point.

$6.175 \times 10^5 = 6.175 \times 100,000 = 617,500.$

$4.1 \times 10^{-5} = 0.000041$

When a number is written in scientific notation, it is written as a decimal with only one digit before the decimal point. This number is multiplied by a power of ten that causes the decimal point to be moved back to its original place.

$6,000,000,000 = 6.0 \times 10^9$

$0.00000000127 = 1.27 \times 10^{-9}$

Scientific Notation Practice

Write the following numbers represented in scientific notation.

1. The distance from the Earth to the sun is 9.296×10^7 miles.

2. The speed of light through air is 2.99×10^8 meters/second.

3. The diameter of a hydrogen atom is 1.06×10^{-9} meters.

4. The mass of an electron is about 9.0×10^{-19} mg.

5. The mass of the Earth is about 5.833×10^{24} kg.

Write the numbers below in scientific notation.

6. The distance from Jupiter to the sun is 483,600,000 miles.

7. The speed of light through diamonds is 124,000,000 meters/second.

8. An average cell is about 0.0025 centimeters long.

9. 0.00000005 of the Earth's atmosphere is helium.

10. The mass of Mars is about 629,481,000,000,000,000,000,000 kg.

The Undoing of Exponents

In mathematics, every operation has an opposite operation that works as an eraser. This eraser operation can undo another. The illustrations below show how the basic operations can be undone.

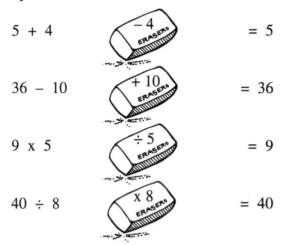

5 + 4   = 5

36 – 10   = 36

9 x 5   = 9

40 ÷ 8   = 40

The opposite of exponents is roots. The sign used to designate roots is $\sqrt{}$. Roots undo or erase exponents as long as they are the same.

$\sqrt[2]{6^2} = 6$

$\sqrt[3]{7^3} = 7$

Exponents erase roots just as roots erase exponents.

$(\sqrt[5]{32})^5 = 32$

$(\sqrt[10]{297})^{10} = 297$

Note: Since square roots are used most frequently, the notation is often simplified.
$$2\sqrt{25} \text{ is the same as } \sqrt{25}.$$

Roots

Use what you know about roots and exponents to complete the problems below.

1a. $5^2 =$ ____

2a. $4^3 =$ ____

1b. $\sqrt{5^2} = \sqrt{\rule{1.5em}{0pt}}$ = ____

2b. $\sqrt[3]{4^3} = \sqrt[3]{\rule{1.5em}{0pt}}$ = ____

3. $\sqrt{49} = \sqrt{\rule{1.5em}{0pt}^2}$ = ____

4. $\sqrt[3]{27} = \sqrt[3]{\rule{1.5em}{0pt}^3}$ = ____

5. $\sqrt[3]{125} = \sqrt[3]{\rule{1.5em}{0pt}^3}$ = ____

6. $\sqrt{100} = \sqrt{\rule{1.5em}{0pt}^2}$ = ____

7. $\sqrt{16} =$ ____

8. $\sqrt{4} =$ ____

9. $\sqrt[3]{8} =$ ____

10. $\sqrt[3]{1,000} =$ ____

11. $\sqrt{81} =$ ____

12. $\sqrt{64} =$ ____

13. $\sqrt[3]{1} =$ ____

14. $\sqrt[3]{216} =$ ____

15. $\sqrt[4]{16} =$ ____

16. $\sqrt[4]{10,000} =$ ____

17. $\sqrt[4]{81} =$ ____

18. $\sqrt[12]{1} =$ ____

Nonperfect Roots

All the roots you have calculated so far were perfect roots. A perfect root is a whole number. Most often, roots don't work out quite as nicely as they did on page 50. Most roots result in decimals that can continue indefinitely. When working with nonperfect roots, a calculator can be used to get a decimal approximation.

$$\sqrt{160} \approx 12.649111$$

Many times, an exact answer must be recorded. When this is the case, roots can be simplified. The number for which you are finding the root can be broken into factors. The most helpful factors are those that result in perfect roots.

$$\sqrt{160} = \sqrt{(16)(10)} = \sqrt{16} \times \sqrt{10} = 4\sqrt{10}$$

Every number, except for prime numbers, can be broken into two or more factors. In simplifying roots, you want the factors to result in perfect roots when possible. If no such factors can be found, the root is as simplified as it can be.

$$\sqrt{10} = \sqrt{(2)(5)}$$

Since 2 and 5 do not result in perfect roots, and there are no other factors of 10 that will produce perfect roots, $\sqrt{10}$ cannot be simplified any further.

Simplify each square root. First, break each of the numbers below into factors. Remember to choose factors that would result in perfect roots when possible. Then simplify.

1. $\sqrt{200}$ = $\sqrt{25 \times 4 \times 2} = 10\sqrt{2}$ 2. $\sqrt{50}$ = _____

3. $\sqrt{48}$ = _____   4. $\sqrt{60}$ = _____

5. $\sqrt{63}$ = _____   6. $\sqrt{128}$ = _____

7. $\sqrt{175}$ = _____   8. $\sqrt{1,350}$ = _____

9. $\sqrt{432}$ = _____   10. $\sqrt{1,008}$ = _____

11. $\sqrt{500}$ = _____   12. $\sqrt{1,000}$ = _____

The Pythagorean Theorem

One of the many practical uses of square roots comes up when working with right triangles. The measures of the sides of right triangles follow a certain property attributed to the great mathematician, Pythagoras. Pythagoras and other mathematicians discovered that the following equation is true for all right triangles:

> **The Pythagorean Theorem**
>
> $$a^2 + b^2 = c^2$$
>
> where *a* and *b* are the measures of the legs of a right triangle and *c* is the measure of the hypotenuse

Use the Pythagorean theorem to solve the problems below. Simplify all roots.

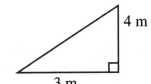

1.

$a^2 + b^2 = c^2$

$3^2 + \underline{\quad}^2 = c^2$

$\underline{\quad} + \underline{\quad} = c^2$

$\underline{\quad} = c^2$

$\sqrt{\underline{\quad}} = \sqrt{c^2}$

$\underline{\quad} = c$

The hypotenuse measures ____ m.

2.

$a^2 + b^2 = c^2$

$\underline{\quad}^2 + \underline{\quad}^2 = c^2$

$\underline{\quad} + \underline{\quad} = c^2$

$\underline{\quad} = c^2$

$\sqrt{\underline{\quad}} = \sqrt{c^2}$

$\underline{\quad} = c$

The hypotenuse measures ____ ft.

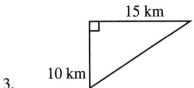

3.

_____

_____

$\underline{\quad} = c$

The hypotenuse measures ____ km.

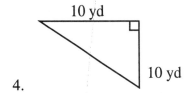

4.

_____

_____

$\underline{\quad} = c$

The hypotenuse measures ____ yd.

Practical Applications

Use the Pythagorean theorem to solve the problems below. Use the pictures or draw some of your own to help you find the right triangle in each problem. Give exact answers unless instructed otherwise.

1. Karyn is making a sail for a boat. She wants the legs of the sail (triangle) to be 5 m and 1 m. What should the measure of the hypotenuse be?

_____

2. Niles is building a ramp next to the steps in the building for those who are in wheelchairs. The steps measure 4 ft tall. He has 10 ft of space next to the steps. How long should he make the ramp?

_____

3. Ken wants to build a ramp to use when skateboarding. He wants his ramp to be 4 ft tall and 5 ft long. Boards wide enough for the ramp cost $4.75 per foot. How much will it cost Ken for the ramp itself not including the support material?

_____

4. Julie wants to build a slide like the one shown above. She wants the slide to be 3.25 m tall and come out 3.5 m. What is the distance kids will slide? (Round to the nearest hundredth.)

_____

5

Working With Variables
Teaching Notes

This chapter includes all the basic skills needed to solve equations. Prior to starting this chapter, students may need a brief review of integer computations and the order of operations.

When students first learn the skills presented in this chapter, they often need varied practice. Regardless of the many practice problems included in this book, it may never be enough for some students. Students often find greater understanding when they see problems in a wide variety of settings.

Manipulatives
Some students learn better by visual or kinesthetic means. These students make a greater connection to items that they can see and touch. They will find manipulatives very helpful.

While teaching the basic skills of solving one-step equations, an analogy between equations and a balance scale is made. If you have access to a balance scale (maybe the science department has one), you can provide your students with hands-on experiences with equations. In addition to using weights, you can use items in the classroom such as pieces of chalk, a calculator, pencils or pens, etc. The weights can be used as constants, and the other objects (chalk, pens, etc.) can be used as variables. Let your students create their own equations by comparing weights on a balance scale.

If you do not have access to a balance scale, students can create their own imaginary scale. To do this, have them cover a small box (such as a raisin box) with plain paper and write an X on it. Gather a large quantity of items that are exactly alike such as paper clips, counters, etc. Let students make up equations using these items and the imaginary balance scale. For example, one such equation might be, $2x = 14$ (clips). So, the weight of $1x$, in this case, would be 7 clips. Using the imaginary scale, the weight of the small box and the value of x can change with each new equation.

Using a Formula

Formulas are used by people in a wide variety of occupations. Scientists, loan officers, computer programmers, and doctors are just a few of the people who use formulas. Formulas can be used in any situation that follows a pattern. Chefs can use a formula to determine the number of eggs they need to make enough omelets to serve any number of people. That formula may look like this:

$$2p = e$$

p = the number of people the chef will serve
e = the number of eggs needed

Formulas are equations that replace numbers that change with letters (called variables). P and e are the variables in the formula above. The number of people to be served and the number of eggs needed can change each time the chef serves omelets. Formulas can be used over and over again with each new situation. No matter how many omelets the chef makes, he or she will always need two eggs for every person he or she serves.

While the formula above is rather simple, most formulas are more involved. In the previous chapter, you learned about one formula that is particularly helpful when working with right triangles. It is called the Pythagorean theorem ($a^2 + b^2 = c^2$). The variables are the measurements of the sides of the triangle. In all the problems in the previous chapter, you plugged in values for the measurements of the legs of a right triangle and solved to find the measurement of the hypotenuse. Each time, the situation involving the right triangle was very different, yet the same formula could be used.

When finding area and volume of shapes and figures, you have also used formulas. For example, the formula for finding the area of a rectangle is: $A = lw$. Area is found by multiplying the measurement of the length by the measurement of the width of a rectangle. The size of the rectangle changes, but the same formula can still be used.

On the following pages, you will find even more formulas used to solve practical problems. Consider what each variable represents. Then plug in the appropriate numbers and solve.

Solving Formulas

Use the formulas shown to solve each problem.

When bowling on a league, bowlers who have an average score under 200 are often given handicaps. A handicap raises a bowler's score to make it possible for bowlers with a range of abilities to compete. A bowler's handicap is calculated using the following formula:

$$H = 0.8(200 - A)$$

H = bowler's handicap
A = bowler's average score

1. If a bowler's average score is 165, what is the bowler's handicap?

    _____

2. How much does a bowler's handicap change if his or her average changes from 165 to 180?

    _____

3. A bowler with an average score of 150 bowls a game with a score of 185. A bowler's handicap is added onto his or her score. Using the average score to calculate handicap, what is this bowler's final score?

    _____

The faster a person drives, the more time it requires to stop. The formula below calculates the approximate distance required for a vehicle to stop on dry pavement.

$$d = 0.042s^2 + 1.1s$$

d = distance in feet
s = speed in miles per hour

4. How long will it take a car to stop if it is traveling at 20 mph?

    _____

5. What is the least amount of space drivers should allow between cars on dry pavement going 55 mph?

    _____

6. What distance do you need to stop if you are riding your bike at a rate of 39,600 ft/hr? (Round to the nearest tenth.)

    _____

7. If a rocket is traveling at a rate of 1,000 miles/min, how many whole miles away from a planet should it start slowing down?

    _____

56   FS-10211 Pre-Algebra Step-by-Step

Solving Formulas continued

When you deposit money in a savings account, you earn an annual rate of interest. The formula below calculates the amount of money that will be in your account after a period of time.

$$T = P(1 + i)^n$$

T = the total amount in your account (deposit plus accumulated interest)

P = the amount of money you deposited, or principal

i = the annual rate of interest

n = the number of years you have left this money untouched

8. If your parents deposited $2,500 in a savings account earning 5% annual interest when you were born, how much money would be in the account on your next birthday?

$T = P(1 + i)^n$

$T = \$2,500 (1 + 0.05)$ ————

$T = \$2,500 (\_\_\_\_)$ ——-

$T = \$2,500 \times _____$

$T = _____$

9. If you deposited $1,000 in a savings account that earned 3.75% interest and never took out any money, how much would be in that account 20 years from now?

_____

Scientists have discovered that crickets can be used as thermometers. The hotter it is, the faster a cricket chirps. The formula below calculates the temperature based on the number of times a cricket chirps each minute.

$$T = \frac{C}{4} + 37$$

T = the approximate temperature (in degrees Fahrenheit)

C = the number of times a cricket chirps in one minute

10. What is the approximate temperature if you hear a cricket chirping 100 times in one minute?

_____

11. Early on a summer's evening, you go outside and hear a cricket chirping 232 times a minute. After dark, you hear a cricket chirping 200 times a minute. How much has the temperature changed?

_____

12. About how many times should you hear a cricket chirp per minute when it is 85°F?

_____

Solving Equations

Most of the work done in algebra involves solving equations similar to the ones shown below.

$$2x + 3y = -17$$

$$15x - 12 = 41$$

$$x^2 + 2x + 1 = 0$$

$$s + 52 = -212$$

$$-14 - 3t = 178$$

Solving equations is similar to detective work. You know some of the pieces, but not all of them. You retrace steps to find more clues. You use what you know to piece together a solution.

In previous chapters, you have seen how operations "undo" each other. Each operation has its opposite. You discovered that roots and exponents are opposites. These operations can be used to "undo" each other.

Undoing an equation is similar to a detective retracing steps. A detective tries to follow the criminal's steps in reverse, hoping it will lead him to the culprit. By working a problem in reverse, you can discover the culprit, the value of the variables.

In this chapter, you'll learn the tricks of the trade in uncovering the values of variables. Just like a detective who uses a variety of techniques to solve the crime, you, as an algebraist, will learn to use a variety of techniques to solve an equation.

One-Step Equations
Addition and Subtraction

As you know, addition and subtraction are opposite operations. In solving all equations, the object is to use opposite operations to isolate the variable. This simply means that you want nothing left but the variable on one side of the equal sign. When you are finished solving, the other side of the equal sign will be the value of the variable. Below and on page 60 are a few examples to help you see this more clearly.

Example 1:

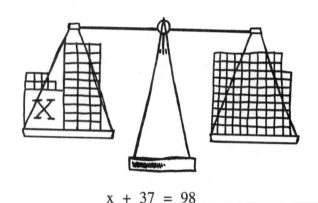

$$x + 37 = 98$$

The scale to the left is a representation of the equation shown below it. Solving this puzzle involves finding the weight of the block labeled X. Solving the equation involves finding the value of the variable x.

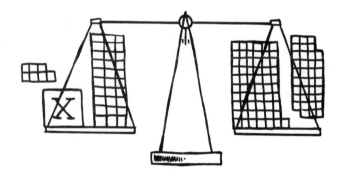

$$x + 37 - 37 = 98 - 37$$

To isolate the x, you need to "undo" the addition of 37. To undo addition, subtract. But, to keep the equation balanced, you must do the same thing on both sides of the equal sign.

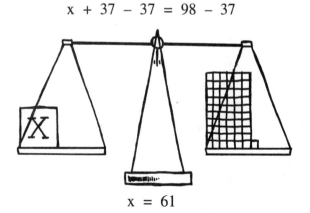

$$x = 61$$

"Undoing" the addition leaves x alone on one side of the equal sign. The number of the other side is the value of x.

To check the answer, substitute 61 for x in the original equation. If the equation is true, the value of x is correct.

$$61 + 37 = 98$$
$$98 = 98 \text{ TRUE}$$

One-Step Equations
Addition and Subtraction continued

Example 2:

$$y - 42 = 112$$

$$y - 42 + 42 = 112 + 42$$

$$y = 154$$

$$154 - 42 = 112$$
$$112 = 112 \text{ TRUE}$$

The opposite of subtraction is addition. To isolate the variable, you must "undo" the subtraction. Then simplify on both sides of the equation.

Example 3:

$$t + -16 + 21 = 3(-27 + 19)$$

$$t + 5 = 3(-27 + 19)$$

$$t + 5 = 3(-8)$$

$$t + 5 = -24$$

Sometimes it is necessary to simplify the equation first. Do all calculations possible on both sides of the equation.

$$t + 5 - 5 = -24 - 5$$

$$t = -29$$

Now you can isolate the variable by undoing the addition.

$$-29 + -16 + 21 = 3(-27 + 19)$$

$$-45 + 21 = 3(-8)$$

$$-24 = -24 \text{ TRUE}$$

Always check your answer by substituting the value of the variable back into the original equation.

Balance is the key to solving any problem.

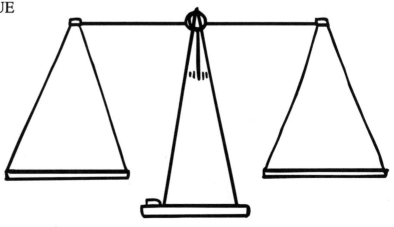

Solving One-Step Equations
Addition and Subtraction

Solve the equations below. Be sure to check your answers.

1. $x - 15 = 28$

   $x - 15 + \underline{\quad} = 28 + \underline{\quad}$

   $x = \underline{\quad}$

   Check:

   $\underline{\quad} - 15 = 28$

   $\underline{\quad} = \underline{\quad}$

2. $t + 63 = 41$

   $t + 63 - \underline{\quad} = 41 - \underline{\quad}$

   $t = \underline{\quad}$

   Check:

   $\underline{\quad} + 63 = 41$

   $\underline{\quad} = \underline{\quad}$

3. $s + 167 = 428$

   $s + 167 \underline{\quad\quad} = 428 \underline{\quad\quad}$

   $s = \underline{\quad}$

   Check:

4. $n - -37 = -62$

   $n - -37 \underline{\quad\quad} = -62 \underline{\quad\quad}$

   $n = \underline{\quad}$

   Check:

5. $p - 87 = -59$

   $p = \underline{\quad}$

   Check:

6. $g + -94 = 14$

   $g = \underline{\quad}$

   Check:

7. $z - 98 + 13 = 7(14 + -8)$

   $z = \underline{\quad}$

   Check:

8. $y + 3(15 - 31) = -115 + 224$

   $y = \underline{\quad}$

   Check:

One-Step Equations
Multiplication and Division

Multiplication and division are also opposite operations. If a variable is multiplied or divided by a number (also called a constant), it can be undone using the opposite operation. Below and on page 63 are some examples of how this works:

Example 1:

The scale to the left is a representation of the equation shown below. Solving this puzzle involves finding the weight of the block labeled X. Solving the equation involves finding the value of the variable x.

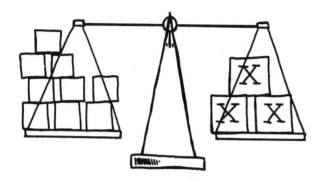

$$3x = 9$$

To isolate the x, you must "undo" the multiplication of 3. To undo multiplication, divide. But, to keep the equation balanced, you must do the same thing on both sides of the equal sign.

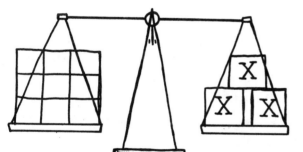

$$\frac{3x}{3} = \frac{9}{3}$$

"Undoing" the addition leaves x alone on one side of the equal sign. The number of the other side is the value of x.

To check the answer, substitute 3 for x in the original equation. If the equation is true, the value of x is correct.

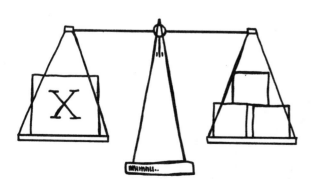

$$x = 3$$

$$3(3) = 9$$
$$9 = 9 \text{ TRUE}$$

One-Step Equations
Multiplication and Division continued

Example 2:

$$x/_{12} = -5$$

$$(12) \, x/_{12} = -5(12)$$

$$x = -60$$

$$^{-60}/_{12} = -5$$

$$-5 = -5 \text{ TRUE}$$

The opposite of division is multiplication. To isolate the variable, you must "undo" the division. Then simplify on both sides of the equation.

Example 3:

$$^3/_{12} \, x = 2^3 - 16$$
$$^1/_4 \, x = 8 - 16$$
$$x/_4 = -8$$

Sometimes it is necessary to simplify the equation first. Do all calculations possible on both sides of the equation.

$$(4) \, x/_4 = -8(4)$$
$$x = -32$$

Now you can isolate the variable by undoing the division.

$$^3/_{12} \, (-32) = 2^3 - 16$$
$$^1/_4 \, x \, ^{-32}/_1 = 8 - 16$$
$$-8 = -8 \text{ TRUE}$$

Always check your answer by substituting the value of the variable back into the original equation.

Solving One-Step Equations Multiplication and Division

Solve the following problems. Remember to check your answers.

1. $3s = 87$

$$\underline{3s} = \underline{87}$$

$s =$ ____

Check:

$3(\underline{\quad}) = 87$

____ = ____

2. $\frac{d}{14} = -12$

$(\underline{\quad})\frac{d}{14} = -12\ (\underline{\quad})$

$d =$ ____

Check:

$\frac{}{14} = -12$

____ = ____

3. $5.7m = 6.84$

$m =$ ____

Check:

4. $\frac{c}{20} = 17$

$c =$ ____

Check:

5. $-\frac{2}{3}x = \frac{5}{8}$

$x =$ ____

Check:

6. $\frac{f}{5.9} = -3.7$

$f =$ ____

Check:

7. $\frac{12}{18}x = 16 - 0.5(48 - 8^2)$

$x =$ ____

Check:

8. $(16 - 28)m = 15 + 7(3)$

$m =$ ____

Check:

How Are Equations Used?

You are well on your way to becoming a great algebraist. You have learned how to solve equations involving one step. Soon you will learn how to handle equations with more than one step. But now, you are probably wondering when you will ever use equations.

Equations are very helpful tools when it comes to solving problems. In most cases, equations are used when you know the final result but you are missing one of the pieces, just like in detective work. A detective knows the final result, the crime committed, but he or she doesn't know some of the pieces, like what led up to the crime or who did it.

Below and on page 66 are some problems in which equations can be used to find the solutions.

Example 1:

John's checking account has a balance of $257.23. Last week, the balance was $157.84. He made a deposit to his account but forgot to write it down. How much did John deposit to his account?

The missing information is the amount of money John deposited. A variable takes the place of missing information. You may want to choose a letter that will help you remember what the variable represents.

$$d = \text{amount of } \textbf{d}\text{eposit}$$

John started with $157.84. He made a deposit that brought his balance up to $257.23. This situation can be described in numbers as well. An equation is a number sentence that describes a situation symbolically.

$$\$157.84 + d = \$257.23$$

Solving the equation will tell John how much money he deposited.

$$\$157.84 + d - \$157.84 = \$257.23 - \$157.84$$
$$d = \$99.39$$

Don't forget to check your work by substituting the answer back into the equation. You should also reread the problem to make sure the answer makes sense. If the equation resulted in a negative answer, in this case, you would know that the equation was incorrect.

$$\$157.84 + \$99.39 = \$257.23$$
$$\$257.23 = \$257.23 \text{ TRUE}$$

John made a $99.39 deposit.

How Are Equations Used? continued

Example 2:

Morgan went on a hiking trip. She wore a pedometer so she knew how far she had hiked. When she stopped for lunch, the pedometer reading was 3,567 yards. After lunch, she finished her hike to her camping spot. The pedometer reading was 9,514 yards. How far did Morgan hike after lunch?

The missing information is the distance Morgan hiked on the second leg of her hike. A variable will present that amount in an equation.

L = distance Morgan hiked after lunch

Morgan hiked 3,567 yards before lunch. Then she hiked the unknown distance. Her total hiking distance was 9,514 yards. The equation to the right describes this symbolically.

$$3{,}567 + L = 9{,}514$$

Solving the equation will tell Morgan how far she hiked after lunch.

$$3{,}567 + L = 9{,}514$$
$$3{,}567 + L - 3{,}567 = 9{,}514 - 3{,}567$$
$$L = 5{,}947$$

$$3{,}567 + 5{,}947 = 9{,}514$$
$$9{,}514 = 9{,}514 \text{ TRUE}$$

Check your answer first by rereading the problem. Does it make sense? Then replace the variable in the equation with the answer you found to make sure the equation is true.

Morgan hiked 5,947 yards after lunch.

Page 67 has more problems similar to the two examples above. You are asked to write an equation that will solve the problem. There are many methods that can be used to solve any problem. You may clearly see another method that will work just as well. This time, use an equation. You can use an alternate method as a way to check your answer.

FS-10211 Pre-Algebra Step-by-Step

Real-Life Equations

For each problem below, decide on the letter you will use for the variable. Describe what the variable represents. Then write an equation that symbolically represents the situation. Solve the equation and check your answer.

1. Luis wrote several checks. Each check was for $25. The overall change in his account was $175. How many $25 checks did Luis write?

   Variable:

   ___ = _____

   Equation:

   _____

   Check:

2. Morgan resumed her hike the following day. According to signs posted along the path, she knew she had to hike 10,367 yards to her next camping spot. When she stopped for lunch, she saw another sign that said her destination was 5,821 yards further. How far did Morgan hike before lunch?

   Variable:

   ___ = _____

   Equation:

   _____

   Check:

3. Carolyn received a puppy for her birthday. She took it to the veterinarian for its shots. At 8 weeks old, her puppy weighed 2.5 lb. Carolyn brought her puppy back to the veterinarian for a checkup when he was 6 months old. At that time, he weighed 14.6 lb. How much weight did Carolyn's puppy gain between visits to the veterinarian?

4. Jay has a generous uncle who has offered to take Jay and his friends to a baseball game and pay for the tickets. Tickets cost $7.95 each. Jay's uncle said he could bring as many friends as he wanted as long as they would all fit in one car. Jay told his uncle that the tickets would cost $39.75. How many people are going to the baseball game?

Two-Step Equations

Remember the order of operations? (<u>P</u>lease <u>E</u>xcuse <u>M</u>y <u>D</u>ear <u>A</u>unt <u>S</u>ally) The order of operations told you in what order you should solve a number sentence having more than one operation. When solving an equation, an algebraist works backwards "undoing" operations to uncover the missing piece. So, when solving an equation involving more than one operation, the order of operations is followed in reverse.

$$5x + 22 = 87$$

Look at the equation above. The equation has two operations—multiplication and addition. To find the value of the variable, you must uncover the variable one layer, or operation, at a time. Following the order of operations in reverse, you know that the first operation to tackle is addition. You know that the opposite of addition is subtraction. To remove the addition layer, subtract.

$$5x + 22 = 87$$
$$5x + 22 - 22 = 87 - 22$$
$$5x = 65$$

The only operation remaining is multiplication. To remove the multiplication, do the opposite, divide.

$$5x = 65$$
$$\tfrac{5x}{5} = \tfrac{65}{5}$$
$$x = 13$$

Checking is done the same way. Plug the answer back into the original equation and see if the equation is true.

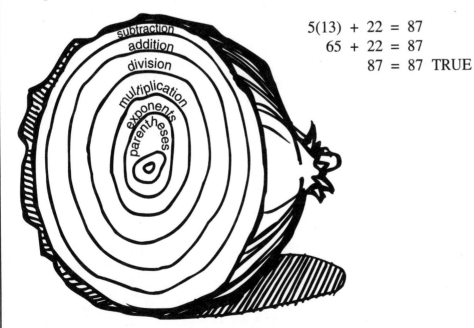

$$5(13) + 22 = 87$$
$$65 + 22 = 87$$
$$87 = 87 \text{ TRUE}$$

Two-Step Equations continued

Below is another example. This time, the equation's operations are division and subtraction. Which layer should you work with first? Following the order of operations in reverse, you know that subtraction must be handled before division.

$$x/17 - 48 = -23$$
$$x/17 - 48 + 48 = -23 + 48$$
$$x/17 = 25$$

Now only one step remains. To isolate the variable, use the opposite operation.

$$(17) \, x/17 = 25(17)$$
$$x = 425$$

Check your answer:

$$^{425}/_{17} - 48 = -23$$
$$25 - 48 = -23$$
$$-23 = -23 \text{ TRUE}$$

As with one-step equations, sometimes equations must be simplified before they are solved. When simplifying an equation, the order of operations is used. Solving an equation requires using the order of operations in reverse.

First simplify:

$$(48 + -59)x - 30 + 2^3 = 17(16 - 4^2)$$
$$-11x - 30 + 8 = 17(16 - 16)$$
$$-11x - 22 = 17(0)$$
$$-11x - 22 = 0$$

Then solve:

$$-11x - 22 + 22 = 0 + 22$$
$$-11x = 22$$
$$^{-11x}/_{-11} = ^{22}/_{-11}$$
$$x = -2$$

Check:

$$(48 + -59)(-2) - 30 + 2^3 = 17(16 - 4^2)$$
$$(-11)(-2) - 30 + 8 = 17(16 - 16)$$
$$22 - 30 + 8 = 17(0)$$
$$-8 + 8 = 0$$
$$0 = 0 \text{ TRUE}$$

Solving Two-Step Equations

Solve the equations below. Remember to use the order of operations in reverse.

1. $3x + 21 = 72$

Check:

2. $\frac{x}{6} - 42 = -16$

Check:

3. $-14n - 67 = -11$

Check:

4. $\frac{21}{18} + -48 = -92$

Check:

5. $-9x + 5(37 - 12) = 98$

Check:

6. $\frac{24x}{8} - 12 + 62 = 4^3$

Check:

Formulas Revisited

When you know how to solve equations, formulas become even more valuable. Look back at the formula problems you solved in the previous chapter. You will notice that you were always solving for the same variable. When you used the Pythagorean theorem ($a^2 + b^2 = c^2$), you were always solving to find c, the measure of the hypotenuse. There are many situations in which you might know the measure of the hypotenuse and you might need to know the measure of one of the legs. Now that you know how to solve equations, you can use the same formula to do this. The examples below and on page 72 show how.

Example 1:

Ned is painting the shutters on his house. He has a 15-foot ladder. If he sets the bottom of the ladder 3 feet from the base of the house, how far up the house will the top of the ladder reach?

In this problem, the length of the hypotenuse and the length of one leg are known. Ned wants to know the length of the remaining leg. Start by plugging into the formula the information you know. Then simplify all that you can.

$$a^2 + b^2 = c^2$$

$$3^2 + b^2 = 15^2$$

$$9 + b^2 = 225$$

Next, isolate the variable. Remember to use the order of operations in reverse. So you must remove the addition layer first.

$$9 + b^2 - 9 = 225 - 9$$
$$b^2 = 216$$

You are left with the exponent. Remember that exponents are "undone" by using roots.

$$\sqrt{b^2} = \sqrt{216}$$
$$b = \sqrt{(9)(4)(6)}$$
$$b = (3)(2)\sqrt{6}$$
$$b = 6\sqrt{6}$$

Formulas Revisited continued

$$T = \frac{C}{4} + 37$$

T = the temperature in degrees Fahrenheit
C = the number of chirps per minute

On page 57, you were asked to determine the number of times a cricket should chirp each minute if the temperature is 85°F. The only way you could solve that problem at the time is by guess and test. Now you can use what you know about solving equations to solve the same problem.

The first step is to plug in the values you know. You know the temperature.

$$T = \frac{C}{4} + 37$$
$$85 = \frac{C}{4} + 37$$

This equation has two operations — addition and division. Using the order of operations in reverse, peel off the addition layer first. Then remove the division layer.

$$85 - 37 = \frac{C}{4} + 37 - 37$$
$$48 = \frac{C}{4}$$
$$(4)48 = \frac{C}{4}(4)$$
$$192 = C$$

When the temperature is 85°F, a cricket will chirp 192 times each minute.

The problems on page 73 require the use of the formulas given below. Choose the correct formula for each situation.

Pythagorean Theorem
$$a^2 + b^2 + c^2$$

Bowler's Handicap
$$H = 0.8(200 - A)$$
H = bowler's handicap
A = bowler's average score

Crickets and Temperature
$$T = \frac{C}{4} + 37$$
T = the temperature in degrees Fahrenheit
C = the number of chirps per minute

Earned Interest
$$T = P(1 + i)^n$$
T = the total amount in your account (deposit plus accumulated interest)
P = the amount of money you deposited, or principal
i = the annual rate of interest
n = the number of years you have left this money untouched

Solving Formulas Revisited

Solve the problems below using the formulas on page 72. Drawing pictures for some problems may be helpful.

1. Jennifer deposited a sum of money in a savings account that earns 8.75% interest. Her account 25 years later has a balance of $8142.01. How much money did Jennifer deposit 25 years ago?

2. A bowler on Christin's league has a handicap of 28. What is this bowler's average?

Jennifer deposited _____.

The bowler's average is _____.

3. The temperature on a hot summer's evening is 87° F. How many times should you hear a cricket chirp each minute?

4. Ben is flying a kite. He has let out the 100-yd string as far as it goes. His kite is flying directly above his house, 20 yd from where he's standing. How far above the ground is the kite?

_____

_____

5. Workers recently erected an electrical tower near your home. One end of 150-m support wires was attached to the top of the tower. The other end was attached 10 m from the base of the tower. How tall is the tower?

6. Maria deposited some money in a 10.25% interest-earning CD. After two years, her CD was worth $607.75. How much money did Maria deposit? (Round to the nearest dollar.)

_____

_____

The Art of Algebra
Teaching Notes

Students who are more visually oriented will be very successful with this chapter. The material in this chapter involves representing equations on a coordinate graph. In addition to plotting points and graphing lines, students will revisit formulas once more. When a formula is mapped out on a graph, it becomes a valuable tool that can be referred to constantly.

Some students need a great amount of practice using the coordinate graph. Below are a few suggestions that will provide students with practice and enjoyment using the coordinate graph. Most of the activities can be done outside of class time so that individual students can get as much practice as they need.

Battleship
You may be familiar with the game, *Battleship*. The game consists of opponents placing various-sized ships on a coordinate grid. The players take turns guessing where on a grid they expect one of their opponent's ships lie. In the commercial game, the grid is labeled with numbers and letters. The grid can just as easily be labeled with integers. When a player has found all the spaces covered by one of his or her opponent's ships, the ship is considered sunk.

In order for your students to play this game, they will each need a sheet of graph paper. On this graph paper, students should make two coordinate graphs—one to keep track of their own ships and one to keep track of their opponent's. They should label the x- and y-axes from -5 to 5. Each player has a fleet of five ships having the following configurations:

XXX   XXXXX   XXXXXXXXXX

  XXX   XXXXX
XXXXXXX   XXXXX
  XXX

The game begins with each player placing his or her ships in horizontal or vertical positions on the coordinate grids. Each X takes the place of one point. Once the ships are in place, players take turns selecting coordinates. For example, player A may think one of player B's ships is on (4, -5). If it is, player B says "hit." If that space is empty, player B says "miss." The first player to sink all of his or her opponent's ships win.

Dot-to-Dot
On page 76, students use ordered pairs to complete a dot-to-dot. Students can gain more practice using the coordinate graph by designing their own dot-to-dots. Suggest that students start by making their own drawing. Then they can list the ordered pairs on a different sheet of paper for a friend to follow.

School Population
Each year, the number of students that attend your school changes. Maybe the change is so small that you don't even recognize it. Over the course of many years, even the slightest changes make a difference. Your school district must stay on top of these changes and even predict the future so that the school doesn't become overcrowded or underpopulated. If the number of students continues to grow, the school district must make plans for adding on another wing or constructing a new school. If there are too few students, the district may decide to bring students from two or more schools together in one building in order to save money. In either case, their decisions will be based on patterns.

Coordinate Plane

You have been graphing on a portion of the coordinate plane for many years. The coordinate plane you have used for graphing is shown to the right below (Graph #1). This is an appropriate graph to use when you are strictly dealing with positive numbers. In many problem solving situations, this is all that is needed. Since you have been introduced to negative numbers, you can now use the entire coordinate plane. The expanded coordinate plane is shown below (Graph #2). With this coordinate plane, you can graph all the real numbers. Even though only integers are shown on each axis, fractions and decimals can be approximated.

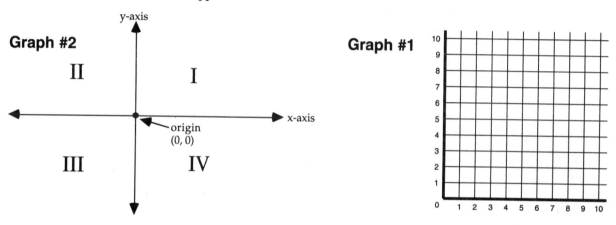

Each section of the coordinate plane is labeled with a Roman numeral. These sections are called quadrants. You are most familiar working with quadrant I which includes all positive numbers.

The first thing you learned to do with graphing is to plot points. Points are described by ordered pairs such as (0, 0), (3, 4), (5, -2), (-4, 0), or (-2, -2). These points are shown on Graph #3.

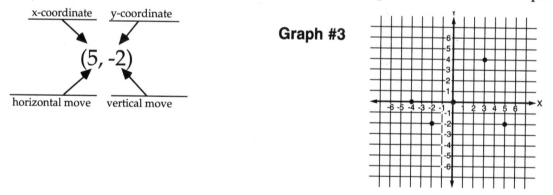

The first number in the ordered pair is called the x-coordinate; the second number is called the y-coordinate. The pair of numbers is a set of directions to a specific point. The directions always start from the origin, the point where the two axes intersect. The sign on a number tells in which direction to move. When a number is positive, move in a positive direction—to the right on the x-axis or up on the y-axis. When a number is negative, move in a negative direction—to the left on the x-axis or down on the y-axis. So, to get to the point described by the ordered pair (5, -2), start at the origin (0). Move 5 units to the right and 2 units down. You should land in quadrant IV.

Practice With the Coordinate Plane

Find each point on the graph. Write the letter corresponding to each point on the appropriate line. When you have found all the points, read the secret message.

The mathematician's answer to the following question is, "Yes!"

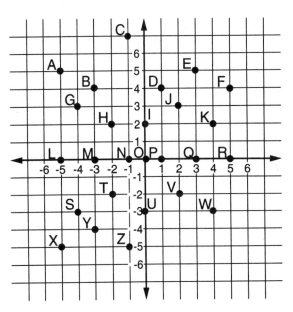

___ ___ ___ ___ ___ ___
(0,2) (-4,-3) (-2,-2)(-2,2) (0,2) (-4,-3)

___ ___ ___ ___ ___ ___ ___ ___
(3,5) (-5,0) (3,5) (2,-2) (-5,5)(-2,-2) (0,0) (5,0)

___ ___ ___ ___ ___
(-4,3) (0,0) (0,2) (-1,0) (-4,3)

___ ___   ___ ___
(0,-3) (1,0)   (0,0) (5,0)

___ ___ ___ ___?
(1,4) (0,0) (4,-3) (-1,0)

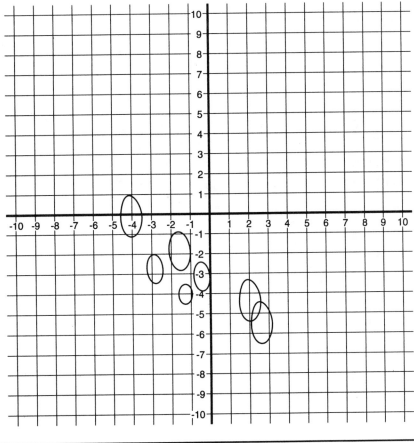

Complete the graph. Plot each of the points below and connect them in order.

(4, -4)
(4, -7.5)
(-5, -2.5)
(-6.5, 3.5)
(4, -3.5)
(4.5, 3.5)
(2, 4.5)
(-4.5, 4.5)
(-6.5, 3.5)

FS-10211 Pre-Algebra Step-by-Step

Lines

Coordinate graphs have more meaningful purposes than designing dot-to-dot designs. They can be quite helpful when analyzing equations. The equations you have worked with so far have had only one variable or unknown. In addition, those equations had only one solution. When equations have more than one variable, they can have an infinite number of solutions. (The word *infinite* means a number so large that it is not even countable, such as the number of grains of sand on a beach.) A coordinate graph helps you see these infinite solutions.

$$x + y = 4$$

The equation above has more than one variable. There are several pairs of numbers that will make the equation true. Just considering whole numbers, the pairs of numbers in the table to the right are all valid solutions.

x	y
0	4
1	3
2	2
3	1
4	0

Now throw in the integers. A few of the additional solutions are to the right. Many more are possible.

x	y
5	-1
15	-11
-467	471
-1,000,000	1,000,004

Finally, include the rest of the real numbers. This includes fractions and decimals. A few of the possibilities are to the right.

x	y
1.5	2.5
6 ⅜	-2 ⅜
-9.37615	13.37615

You are probably beginning to see that there are so many different solutions possible that there would be no way of listing them all. You are correct. The number of possible solutions is infinite. A line is also infinite. You may remember that a line continues forever in opposite directions. A line is created by an infinite number of points. What a better way to represent the solutions of an equation!

The solutions for an equation with two variables can be shown on the graph by writing the solutions as ordered pairs. For example, the first solution listed in the table above can be described as (0, 4). This point can easily be located on a graph. To create a line that represents <u>all</u> the solutions for an equation, simply plot a few points and connect them. Every point along the line will be another valid solution for the equation.

Lines continued

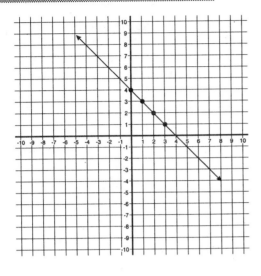

$$x + y = 4$$

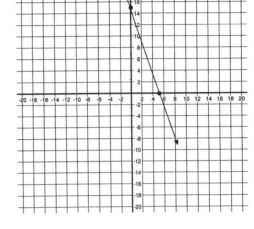

$$3x + y = 15$$

The graph of the equation $x + y = 4$ (left) lies in three quadrants—I, II, and IV. None of the solutions can be found in quadrant III. Why? Quadrant III has pairs of numbers that are both negative. There are no pairs of negative numbers that add up to a positive number.

Look at the equation $3x + y = 15$. This time, all the possible solutions are not listed. All of the solutions don't need to be found. All you need to do to plot the equation is find three to five points, plot them on a graph, and draw the line. The line gives you all the possible solutions to the equation. To find some points, just pick any number for one of the variables. Then solve to find the value of the other variable. Choosing smaller numbers like 1 and 0 makes solving very simple.

$$3x + y = 15$$

Choose a number for x, for example 0.

One valid solution is x = 0, y = 15.
So one point on the line is (0, 15).

$$3x + y = 15$$
$$3(0) + y = 15$$
$$0 + y = 15$$
$$y = 15$$

What happens when you make y = 0?

Another valid solution is x = 5, y = 0.
So another point on the line is (5, 0).

$$3x + y = 15$$
$$3x + 0 = 15$$
$$3x = 15$$
$$x = 5$$

Find one more point. This time use a negative number. When x = -1, y = 18. So a third point on the line is (-1, 18).
The graph of this line is shown to the right above.

$$3x + y = 15$$
$$3(-1) + y = 15$$
$$-3 + y = 15$$
$$-3 + 3 + y = 15 + 3$$
$$y = 18$$

Graphing Lines

Complete each table below by substituting the values of x and y into the equations. Then graph each line.

1. x + y = 5

x	y
0	—
—	2
—	0

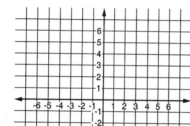

2. 6x – y = 2

x	y
1	—
0	—
—	0

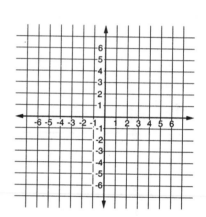

3. -2x + 4y = 0

x	y
-2	—
—	0
—	1

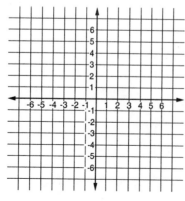

4. ½ = -4x + 2

x	y
0	—
—	-4
—	0

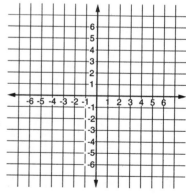

FS-10211 Pre-Algebra Step-by-Step

Graphing More Lines

Graph each of the following lines on the graph below. Find and label at least three points on each line.

1. $2y - 3x = 6$

2. $9x + 6y = 54$

3. $y = \frac{2}{3}x - 2$

4. $4x + 6y = -12$

5. $y - 3 = 0$

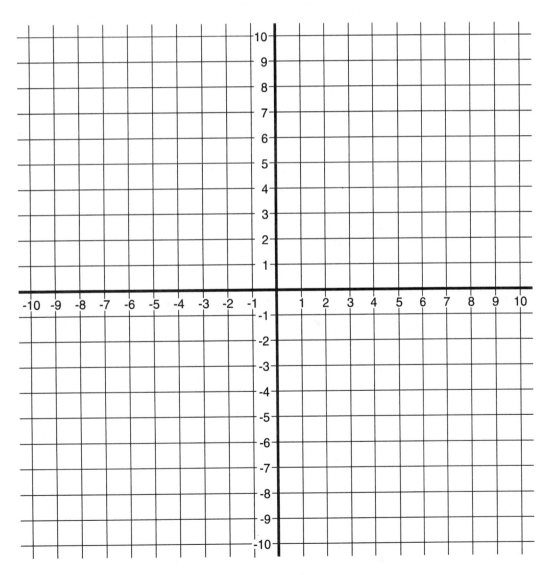

Graphing Formulas

Name _____

When formulas have only two variables, they can be drawn on a graph. This can be very helpful. Instead of reworking the formula each time it is needed, a result can be found on the graph.

In the previous chapter, you solved problems using the formula below. This formula predicts the temperature based on the number of times a cricket chirps every minute. Put this equation on a graph.

$$T = \frac{C}{4} + 37$$

To do this, you must first decide which variable should go on the horizontal (or x) axis and which should go on the vertical (or y) axis. The variable placed on the horizontal axis is an independent variable. The variable on the the vertical axis is dependent—its value is dependent on the other variable. Consider the situation in which the formula above is used. Does the temperature depend on the number of chirps a cricket makes? In other words, does the temperature change based on the number of chirps a cricket makes? No. Does the number of chirps a cricket makes depend on the temperature? In other words, does the cricket change the number of chirps it makes as the temperature changes? Yes. The cricket chirps depend on the temperature. So, the variable C depends on the variable T. This means that C, the dependent variable, should go on the vertical axis, and T, the independent variable, should go on the horizontal axis.

Before this equation is plotted on a graph, make some observations. In what quadrants should this equation lie? In the first quadrant, both variables are positive. Positive chirps and positive temperatures make sense. Should there be negative chirps and/or negative temperatures? Crickets do not chirp in the winter, so negative temperatures are not needed. Negative chirps do not make sense. So, even though the line could continue into other quadrants, all that is needed for this formula is the first quadrant.

Graphing this formula is the same as graphing any line. Pick values to substitute for one of the variables and solve for the other. In this case, it is easiest to plug in values for C and solve for T. Choose values that are easy to work with. Multiples of four will make solving easier. The graph is on page 82.

T	C
37	0
47	40
57	80

FS-10211 Pre-Algebra Step-by-Step

Name _____

Graphing Formulas continued

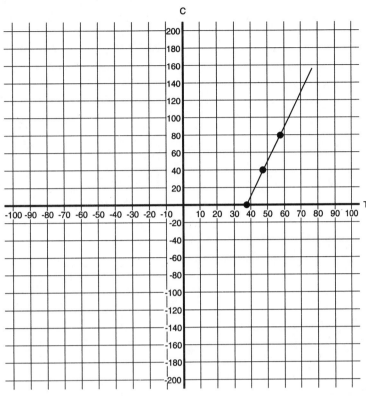

Having the graph will make it possible to solve many problems involving the formula without having to rework the formula over and over again. Answer the following questions using the graph above.

1. What is the lowest temperature at which you may hear a cricket chirping?

   _____

2. Which variable increases at the greatest rate?

   _____

3. What's the approximate temperature when a cricket is chirping 60 times each minute?

   _____

4. About how many times should a cricket be chirping each minute if the temperature is 50°F?

   _____

5. What is the least number of times you would expect to hear a cricket chirp each minute when the temperature is 95°F?

   _____

6. Does a cricket stop chirping when the temperature goes above 100°F?

   _____

Graphing More Formulas

Graph each of the formulas below. Then answer the questions by referring to the graph.

In the previous chapter, you worked with a formula used to determine a bowler's handicap. Cindy is a bowling league manager. It would be helpful for her to have a graph of the formula.

$$H = 0.8(200 - A)$$

H = bowler's handicap
A = bowler's average score

1. Graph the formula below.

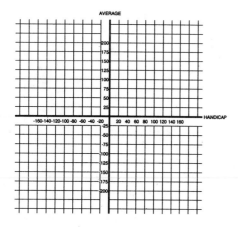

2. What is the highest score for which a bowler receives a handicap?

_____

3. What handicap should a bowler receive if his or her average score is 100?

_____

4. What is the highest handicap any bowler could receive? Do you think it is probable that any bowler receive this handicap?

_____

Each afternoon, Ken walks a two-mile mountain trail. He wonders how his speed changes each day. The following formula can help:

$$D = RT$$

D = distance (2 miles or 10,560 feet)
R = rate
T = time

5. Graph the equation, $10,560 = RT$.

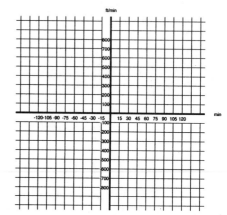

6. Is the graph of this equation a line or a curve?

_____

7. Can R or T ever equal zero?

_____

8. If it takes Ken 60 minutes to walk the trail, about how fast is he walking on average?

_____

9. Ken's goal is to walk at a rate of 500 ft/min. In how much time should he complete the trail when he reaches this goal?

_____

Predicting Graphs—y = 0

By looking at a few basic graphs, you can learn to predict what the graph of a line will look like. There are three basic lines. Consider each one individually. Alter each line slightly and check the results. By analyzing the results, you can predict how another change might affect the graph.

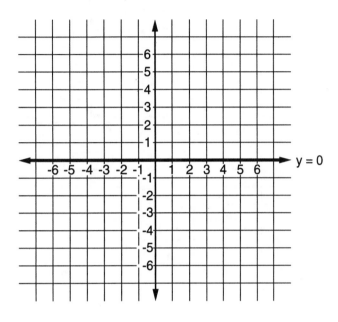

1. Give the coordinates for three points that lie on the line y = 0.

   _____

2. On the line y = 0, no matter what the value of x is, y always equals _____ .

3. Graph the equation y = 5.

4. How did changing the equation affect the line? In other words, how is the line y = 5 different from the line y = 0?

   _____

5. Graph the equation y = -2.

6. How did changing the equation affect the line?

   _____

7. Describe all lines of the form *y = some number*.

   _____

Predicting Graphs—x = 0

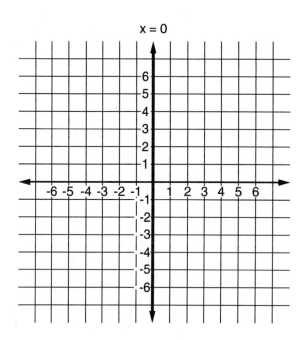

1. Name three points that lie on the line x = 0.

_____

2. Regardless of the value of y, x always equals _____ on the line x = 0.

3. Describe what you expect the line x = 3 to look like. Where will it be on the graph?

_____

4. Graph the line x = 3. Were your predictions correct?

_____

5. Describe the move you'd make to line x = 0 to make it the line x = -2.

_____

Predicting Graphs—y = x

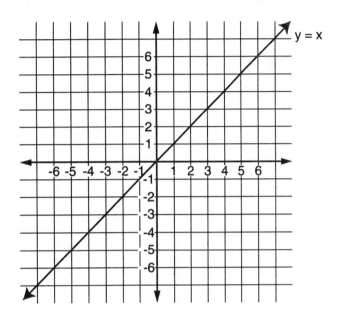

1. Name three points that lie on the line y = x.

   _____

2. Graph the line y = x + 3. How is y = x + 3 different from y = x?

   _____

3. Describe how you predict the line y = x + 5 will look.

   _____

4. Graph the line y = x + 5. Were your predictions correct?

   _____

5. Graph the line y = 2x. How does the coefficient 2 affect the line?

   _____

6. Graph the line y = ⅔x. How does the fractional coefficient affect the line?

   _____

7. Graph the line y = -2x. How does the negative coefficient affect the line?

   _____

Predicting Graphs—y = x continued

For each of the equations below, first describe how you expect the line to look. Then graph the line.

8. y = -⅔x

_____

_____

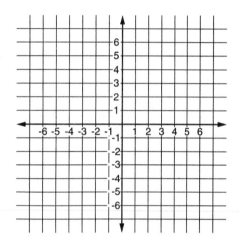

9. y = -5x

_____

_____

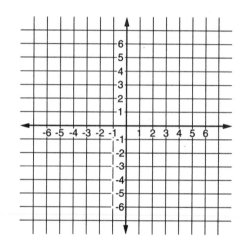

10. y = ½x

_____

_____

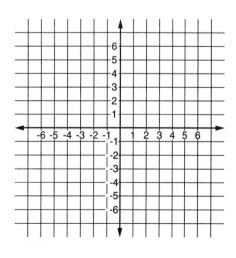

11. y = ½x − 2

_____

_____

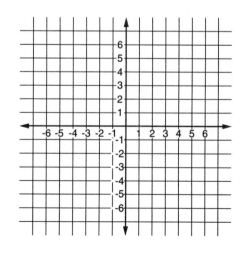

Organizing Data

Find the total student enrollment for your school for the past twenty years. If you are unable to find this data for twenty years, find the enrollment totals for as many years as possible. Record the data in the table, then graph the data.

Year	Student Enrollment

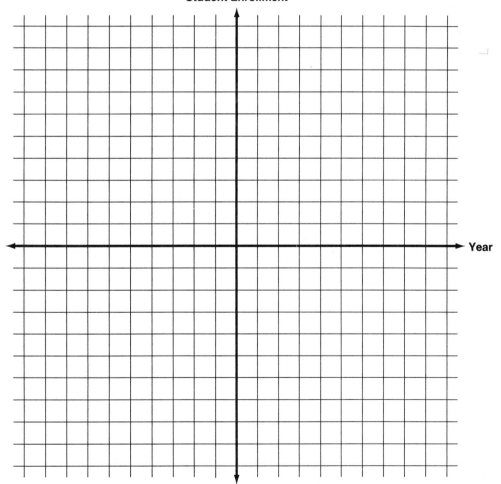

Student Enrollment

Year

Analyzing Data

Use the data in your graph on page 88 to answer the following questions.

1. On the average, is the population of your school increasing or decreasing?

   _____

2. Starting with the earliest year for which you have data, how long did it take student enrollment to increase (or decrease) by 5%?

   _____

3. How long did it take for the next 5% increase (or decrease)?

   _____

4. How many years do you think it will be before student enrollment increases (or decreases) another 5% from its current level?

   _____

5. Describe any pattern you can see in the way the enrollment of your school changes.

   _____

   _____

6. What could be the reasons for the patterns you see? Have any new schools been built or any schools combined over the years for which you have data? Has anything happened that would cause a large number of people to move to or from the area?

   _____

   _____

   _____

7. Assume school enrollment will continue to increase or decrease in the same way that it has in the past. Make a prediction. In how many years will the school district have to make some major changes, such as adding more rooms or closing down a school, due to the changed enrollment? Explain your answer.

   _____

   _____

   _____

   _____

Answer Key

Symbols Practice   page 4
1. 5(6) = 30
2. 467 > 16 (≥ and ≠ are also correct.)
3. 67 < 72 (≤ and ≠ are also correct.)
4. |-4| = 4 (<, ≤, and ≠ are also correct.)
5. 87.995 ≈ 88 (<, ≤, and ≠ are also correct.)
6. 14 • 47 = 658
7. 92 ≥ 92
8. 14.141141 . . . = 14.$\overline{141}$
9. 45 = 9(5)
10. 620 = 620 (≥ and ≤ are also correct.)
11. 56.$\overline{143}$
12. 33 ≤ 42 (< and ≠ are also correct.)
13. 5.$\overline{165}$
14. 28
15. 15
16. Accept any number less than or equal to 34.6.
17. Accept any number greater than or equal to 91.
18. 52
19. 21
20. 583
21. Accept any number greater than 43.
22. 32

The Number Maze   page 5

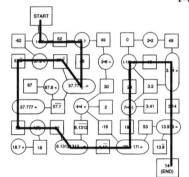

Numbers Practice   pages 8-9
Students should circle the following numbers:
1. -57, ⅔, 0, 0.5
2. ⅜, 1.6, -2
3. ¹⁵⁄₂₁, -12.75
4. π
Students' answers will vary for questions 5 - 8.

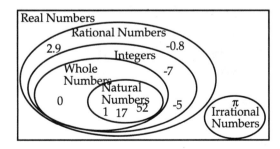

Properties   page 12
Students should see that it is easier to multiply the 4 by each number individually in the first case. The individual multiplication problems are simple enough for mental work. This also makes the addition easier.
In the second example, it's easier to subtract first and then multiply.
The difference is a number that is much easier to multiply mentally than the original two numbers were.

Properties Practice   page 13
1. 117 + 96 + 83 + 24 =   Distributive Property
    117 + 83 + 96 + 24 =   Commutative Property
    200 + 120 = 320
2. (22 + 28) + 57 - 57 =   Associative Property
    50 + 0 = 50   Additive Identity Property or
    Additive Inverse Property
3. 0; Multiplication Property of Zero
4. x; Additive Identity Property
5. 2,200; Commutative Property
6. 2,200; Associative Property
7. 371; Multiplicative Inverse Property
8. 5,180; Distributive Property
9. y; Additive Inverse Property

Algebraic Lingo Practice   page 15

Across	Down
1. variable	2. associative
4. sum	3. expression
5. product	6. inequality
7. term	8. commutative
10. solution	9. constant
11. real	
12. rational	
13. integers	
14. equation	
15. coefficient	

Order of Operations Practice   page 18
The coded message is, "Good drivers and good mathematicians master the rules of the road."

Investigating Integer Addition   page 23
1. -2   6. -5
2. 2   7. -5
3. -12   8. 0
4. 7   9. 12
5. 5   10. 0

Addition Investigation Follow-Up   page 24
Students should discover the following:
1. The two groups join together and remain positive.
2. The two groups join together and remain negative.
3. Subtract the number of members of each group to find the remaining number of chips. These chips are negative.
4. Subtract the number of members of each group to find the remaining number of chips. These chips are positive.
5. No chips remain.
6. The same patterns will be true when adding integers.

Adding in Real-Life Situations   page 25
1. -50 + 23 = -27
2. -15 + 25 = 10
3. 35 + -10 = 25
4. -3,000 + 1,200 = -1,800
5. -250 + -125 = -375
6. -5 + 11 = 6
7. 56 + -7 = 49
8. 57 + -90 = -33

Investigating Integer Subtraction   page 28
1. 5 + -3 = 2
2. -7 + 5 = -2
3. 2 + -5 = -3
4. -4 + 6 = 2
5. -6 + -3 = -9
6. 4 + 1 = 5
7. 2 + 5 = 7
8. -8 + -3 = -11
9. -10 + -6 = -16
10. 6 + -14 = -8

Subtraction Investigation Follow-Up page 29

Students should discover the following:
1. The numbers of the two groups can be subtracted. The answer has the same sign as the group members.
2. The numbers of the two groups can be subtracted. The answer has the opposite sign as the group members.
3. The numbers of the two groups can be added. The answer is positive.
4. The numbers of the two groups can be added. The answer is negative.

Subtracting in Real-Life Situations page 30
1. $-1 - 8 = -9$
2. $-500 - 100 = -600$
3. $75 - 37 = 38$
4. $117 - 123 = -6$
5. $-6 - 25 = -31$
6. $4,120 - 1,375 = 2,745$
7. $5 - 7 = -2$
8. $5 - 9 = -4$

Making Sense of Integer Multiplication and Division page 33
1. The sign will always be negative.
2. The sign will always be negative.
3. Multiplication and division are opposite operations. A division problem can be changed to a multiplication problem by multiplying by the reciprocal of the divisor.
4. The sign should be positive in both cases.
5. Answers will vary.
6. -24
7. -21
8. 7
9. 45
10. -126
11. -11

Multiplying and Dividing in Real-Life Situations page 34
1. $-25 \times 60 = -1,500$
2. $-144 \div 8 = -18$
3. $-37 \times 7 = -259$
4. $3 \times 6 = 18$
5. $-1,725 \div -75 = 23$
6. $-24 \div 4 = -6$
7. $-16 \times 6 = -96$
8. $-8 \div -2 = 4$

Solving Problems With Decimals page 37
1. $103.2 + -3.7 = 99.5$
2. $98.7 + -3.8 = 94.9$
3. $-500 + -200 + 147.86 = -552.14$
4. $-45.52 + -66.12 + -17.85 + 115.22 = -14.27$
5. $-648.6 \div -27.6 = 23.5$
6. $30 \times -27.6 = -828$
7. $-0.25 \times 3 \times 5 = -3.75$
8. $4 \times -3.95 + 20 = 4.20$

Solving Problems With Fractions page 39
1. $26\,\% + -3\,\% = 22\,\%$
2. $236\,\% + 1,000 + -1,200 = 36\,\%$
3. $(15)\% + (15)\% = 4$
4. $100 + -6\,\% + -4\,\%, + -2\,\% + -8 + -4\,\% = 73\,\%$
5. $2\,\% + \% + \% + \% + -1\% = \%$
6. $-2,752 \div -107\,\% = 25\%$

Exponents page 45
1. 5
2. $3 \times 3 \times 3$
3. 6
4. 1
5. 5
6. 3,125
7. $2^1 = 2^2 \div 2 = 2$
8. $2^0 = 2^1 \div 2 = 1$
9. $2^{-2} = 2^{-1} \div 2 = 2^{-1} \times \tfrac{1}{2} = \tfrac{1}{4} = \tfrac{1}{2^2}$
10. $2^{-3} = 2^{-2} \div 2 = 2^{-2} \times \tfrac{1}{2} = \tfrac{1}{8} = \tfrac{1}{2^3}$
11. When any base has a negative exponent, it is equal to a fraction: 1 over the base to a positive exponent.

Patterns of Powers page 46
1. 1,000
2. 100
3. 10
4. 1
5. 0.001
6. 0.0001
7. 0.00001
8. When the exponent is positive, it describes the number of zeros behind the 1 in the answer. When the exponent is negative, there is one less zero than the absolute value of the exponent in front of the 1 in the answer.
9. The decimal point moves over one additional place each time the exponent increases or decreases by one. The decimal point moves to the left when the exponent is negative and to the right when the exponent is positive.
10. This pattern is only true for powers of ten. Accept any reasonable explanation.

Scientific Notation Practice page 48
1. 92,960,000 miles
2. 299,000,000 meters/second
3. 0.00000000106 meter
4. 0.0000000000000000009 mg
5. 5,833,000,000,000,000,000,000,000 kg
6. 4.837×10^8 miles
7. 1.25×10^8 meters/second
8. 2.5×10^{-3} cm
9. 5.0×10^{-8}
10. 6.29481×10^{23} kg

Roots page 50
1a. 25
1b. $\sqrt{25} = 5$
2a. 64
2b. $\sqrt[3]{64} = 4$
3. $\sqrt{7^2} = 7$
4. $\sqrt[3]{3^3} = 3$
5. $\sqrt[3]{5^3} = 5$
6. $\sqrt{10^2} = 10$
7. 4
8. 2
9. 2
10. 10
11. 9
12. 8
13. 1
14. 6
15. 2
16. 10
17. 3
18. 1

Nonperfect Roots page 51
1. $\sqrt{25 \times 4 \times 2} = 10\sqrt{2}$
2. $\sqrt{25 \times 2} = 5\sqrt{2}$
3. $\sqrt{16 \times 3} = 4\sqrt{3}$
4. $\sqrt{4 \times 15} = 2\sqrt{15}$
5. $\sqrt{9 \times 7} = 3\sqrt{7}$
6. $\sqrt{16 \times 4 \times 2} = 8\sqrt{2}$
7. $\sqrt{25 \times 7} = 5\sqrt{7}$
8. $\sqrt{25 \times 9 \times 6} = 15\sqrt{6}$
9. $\sqrt{16 \times 9 \times 3} = 12\sqrt{3}$
10. $\sqrt{16 \times 9 \times 7} = 12\sqrt{7}$
11. $\sqrt{100 \times 5} = 10\sqrt{5}$
12. $\sqrt{100 \times 10} = 10\sqrt{10}$

The Pythagorean Theorem   **page 52**

1. $3^2 + 4^2 = c^2$
   $9 + 16 = c^2$
   $25 = c^2$
   $\sqrt{25} = \sqrt{c^2}$
   $5 = c$
   The hypotenuse measures 5 m.

2. $9^2 + 15^2 = c^2$
   $81 + 225 = c^2$
   $306 = c^2$
   $\sqrt{306} = \sqrt{c^2}$
   $3\sqrt{34} = c$
   The hypotenuse measures $3\sqrt{34}$ ft.

3. $10^2 + 15^2 = c^2$
   $100 + 225 = c^2$
   $325 = c^2$
   $\sqrt{325} = \sqrt{c^2}$
   $5\sqrt{13} = c$
   The hypotenuse measures $5\sqrt{13}$ km.

4. $10^2 + 10^2 = c^2$
   $100 + 100 = c^2$
   $200 = c^2$
   $\sqrt{200} = \sqrt{c^2}$
   $10\sqrt{2} = c$
   The hypotenuse measures $10\sqrt{2}$ yd.

Practical Applications   **page 53**

1. $\sqrt{26}$
2. $\sqrt{116} = 2\sqrt{29}$
3. Ken needs about 6 ½ feet of board which will cost $30.88.
4. 4.78 m

Solving Formulas   **pages 56-57**

1. 28
2. The bowler's handicap decreases by 12.
3. 225
4. 38.8 ft
5. 187.55 ft
6. 10.6 ft
7. 28,649 miles
8. The answer will vary depending on the student's age. Here are some possible answers.
   Age = 11 n = 12 T = $4,489.64
   Age = 12 n = 13 T = $4,714.12
   Age = 13 n = 14 T = $4,949.83
   Age = 14 n = 15 T = $5,197.32
   Age = 15 n = 16 T = $5,457.19
9. $2,088.15
10. 62°F
11. The temperature has gone down 8°F.
12. 192 chirps per minute

Solving One-Step Equations—Addition and Subtraction   **page 61**

1. $x - 15 + 15 = 28 + 15$
   $x = 43$
   $43 - 15 = 28$
   $28 = 28$
2. $t + 63 - 63 = 41 - 63$
   $t = -22$
   $-22 + 63 = 41$
   $41 = 41$
3. $s + 167 - 167 = 428 - 167$
   $s = 261$
   $261 + 167 = 428$
   $428 = 428$
4. $n - -37 + -37 = -62 + -37$
   $n = -99$
   $-99 - -37 = -62$
   $-62 = -62$

5. $p - 87 + 87 = -59 + 87$
   $p = 28$
   $28 - 87 = -59$
   $-59 = -59$
6. $g + -94 - -94 = 14 - -94$
   $g = 108$
   $108 + -94 = 14$
   $14 = 14$
7. $z - 85 = 7(6)$
   $z - 85 = 42$
   $z - 85 + 85 = 42 + 85$
   $z = 127$
   $127 - 98 + 13 = 7(14 + -8)$
   $29 + 13 = 7(6)$
   $42 = 42$
8. $y + 3(-16) = 109$
   $y + -48 = 109$
   $y + -48 - -48 = 109 - -488$
   $y = 157$
   $157 + 3(15 - 31) = -115 + 224$
   $157 + 3(-16) = 109$
   $157 + -48 = 109$
   $109 = 109$

Solving One-Step Equations—Multiplication and Division   **page 64**

1. $\frac{3f}{3} = \frac{87}{3}$
   $f = 29$
   $3(29) = 87$
   $87 = 87$
2. $(14)\frac{d}{14} = -12(14)$
   $d = -168$
   $\frac{-168}{14} = -12$
   $-12 = -12$
3. $\frac{5.7m}{5.7} = \frac{6.84}{5.7}$
   $m = 1.2$
   $5.7(1.2) = 6.84$
   $6.84 = 6.84$
4. $(20)\frac{c}{20} = 17(20)$
   $c = 340$
   $\frac{340}{20} = 17$
   $17 = 17$
5. $(-\frac{3}{2})-\frac{2}{3}x = \frac{5}{8}(-\frac{3}{2})$
   $x = -\frac{15}{16}$
   $-\frac{2}{3}(-\frac{15}{16}) = \frac{5}{8}$
   $\frac{5}{8} = \frac{5}{8}$
6. $(5.9)\frac{f}{5.9} = -3.7(5.9)$
   $f = -21.83$
   $\frac{-21.83}{5.9} = -3.7$
   $-3.7 = -3.7$
7. $\frac{2}{3}x = 16 - 0.5(48 - 64)$
   $\frac{2}{3}x = 16 - 0.5(-16)$
   $\frac{2}{3}x = 16 - -8$
   $\frac{2}{3}x = 24$
   $(\frac{3}{2})\frac{2}{3}x = 24(\frac{3}{2})$
   $x = 36$
   $\frac{12}{18}(36) = 16 - 0.5(48 - 8^2)$
   $\frac{2}{3}(36) = 16 - 0.5(48 - 64)$
   $24 = 16 - 0.5(-16)$
   $24 = 16 - -8$
   $24 = 24$
8. $-12m = 15 + 21$
   $-12m = 36$
   $\frac{-12m}{-12} = \frac{36}{-12}$
   $m = -3$
   $(16 - 28)-3 = 15 + 7(3)$
   $(-12)-3 = 15 + 21$
   $36 = 36$

1. c = the number of checks Luis wrote
   $25c = $175
   c = 7
   $25(7) = $175
   $175 = $175 TRUE
   Luis wrote 7 checks.
2. h = the number of yards Morgan hiked before lunch
   h + 5,821 = 10,367
   h = 4,546
   4,546 + 5,821 = 10,367
   10,367 = 10,367 TRUE
   Morgan hiked 4,546 yd before lunch.
3. w = the amount of weight the puppy gained
   2.5 + w = 14.6
   w = 12.1
   2.5 + 12.1 = 14.6
   14.6 = 14.6 TRUE
   Carolyn's puppy gained 12.1 lb.
4. t = the number of people going to the baseball game
   $7.95t = $39.75
   t = 5
   $7.95 (5) = $39.75
   $39.75 = $39.75
   Five people are going to the baseball game.

Solving Two-Step Equations   page 70

1. $3x + 21 - 21 = 72 - 21$
   $3x = 51$
   $\frac{3x}{3} = \frac{51}{3}$
   $x = 17$
   $3(17) + 21 = 72$
   $51 + 21 = 72$
   $72 = 72$ TRUE
2. $\frac{x}{6} - 42 + 42 = -16 + 42$
   $\frac{x}{6} = 26$
   $(6)\frac{x}{6} = 26(6)$
   $x = 156$
   $\frac{156}{6} - 42 = -16$
   $26 - 42 = -16$
   $-16 = -16$ TRUE
3. $-14n - 67 + 67 = -11 + 67$
   $-14n = 56$
   $\frac{-14n}{-14} = \frac{56}{-14}$
   $n = -4$
   $-14(-4) - 67 = -11$
   $56 - 67 = -11$
   $-11 = -11$ TRUE
4. $\frac{t}{9} + -48 - -48 = -92 - -48$
   $\frac{t}{9} = -44$
   $(9)\frac{t}{9} = -44(9)$
   $t = -396$
   $\frac{(2)(-396)}{18} + -48 = -92$
   $\frac{-792}{18} + -48 = -92$
   $-44 + -48 = -92$
   $-92 = -92$ TRUE
5. $-9x + 5(25) = 98$
   $-9x + 125 = 98$
   $-9x + 125 - 125 = 98 - 125$
   $-9x = -27$
   $\frac{-9x}{-9} = \frac{-27}{-9}$
   $x = 3$
   $-9(3) + 5(37 - 12) = 98$
   $-27 + 5(25) = 98$
   $-27 + 125 = 98$
   $98 = 98$ TRUE
6. $-3x + 50 = 64$
   $-3x + 50 - 50 = 64 - 50$
   $-3x = 14$
   $\frac{-3x}{3} = \frac{14}{3}$
   $x = \frac{-14}{3} = -4\frac{2}{3}$
   $[(24)\frac{-14}{3}] \div -8 - 12 + 62 = 4^3$
   $\frac{-112}{8} + 50 = 64$
   $14 + 50 = 64$
   $64 = 64$ TRUE

1. $8,142.01 = P(1 + 0.0875)^{25}$
   $8,142.01 = 8.142P$
   $\frac{$8142.01}{8.142} = \frac{8.142P}{8.142}$
   $1,000 = P$
   Jennifer deposited $1,000.
2. $28 = 0.8(200 - A)$
   $\frac{28}{0.8} = \frac{0.8(200-A)}{0.8}$
   $35 = 200 - A$
   $35 - 200 = 200 - 200 - A$
   $-165 = -A$
   $165 = A$
   The bowler's average is 165.
3. $87 = \frac{C}{4} + 37$
   $87 - 37 = \frac{C}{4} + 37 - 37$
   $50 = \frac{C}{4}$
   $(4)50 = \frac{C}{4}(4)$
   $200 = C$
   A cricket should chirp 200 times each minute.
4. $20^2 + b^2 = 100^2$
   $400 + b^2 = 10,000$
   $400 - 400 + b^2 = 10,000 - 400$
   $b^2 = 9,600$
   $\sqrt{b^2} = \sqrt{9600}$
   $b = \sqrt{(100)(16)(6)}$
   $b = (10)(4)\sqrt{6}$
   $b = 40\sqrt{6}$
   The kite is flying $40\sqrt{6}$ yards above the ground.
5. $10^2 + b^2 = 150^2$
   $100 + b^2 = 22,500$
   $100 - 100 + b^2 = 22,500 - 100$
   $b^2 = 22,400$
   $\sqrt{b^2} = \sqrt{22400}$
   $b = \sqrt{(100)(16)(14)}$
   $b = (10)(4)\sqrt{14}$
   $b = 40\sqrt{14}$
   The electrical tower is $40\sqrt{14}$ m tall.
6. $607.75 = P(1 + 0.1025)^2$
   $607.75 = 1.216P$
   $\frac{$607.75}{1.216} = \frac{1.216P}{1.216}$
   $500 = P$
   Maria deposited $500.

Practice With the Coordinate Plane   page 76

After finding all the points, the students should have decoded the following question: "Is this elevator going up or down?"

Graphing Lines   page 79

1.

x	y
0	5
3	2
5	0

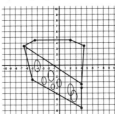

Graphing Lines continued   page 79

2.
x	y
1	4
0	-2
⅓	0

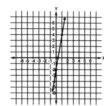

3.
x	y
-2	-1
0	0
2	1

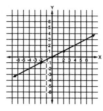

4.
x	y
0	4
1	-4
½	0

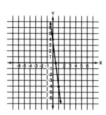

Graphing More Lines   page 80

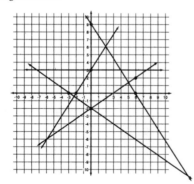

Graphing Formulas continued   page 82
1. about 38 to 40 degrees
2. C increases much quicker than T.
3. about 52°F
4. about 52 times each minute
5. 232 chirps
6. No.

Graphing More Formulas   page 83
1.

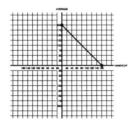

2. 199
3. 80
4. The highest handicap is 160. To receive this handicap, a bowler would have to have an average of 0 which is almost impossible.
5.

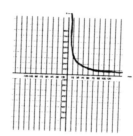

6. The graph is a curve.
7. The rate and time can never equal 0.
8. Ken is walking about 175 ft/min.
9. It should take Ken about 22 min.

Predicting Graphs—y = 0   page 84
1. Any three points with a y value of 0
2. 0
3.

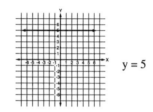

y = 5

4. The line moved up 5 units.
5.

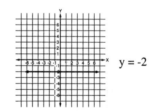

y = -2

6. The line shifted down 2 units.
7. These lines are always horizontal, and they cross the y-axis at the *some number.'*

Predicting Graphs—x = 0   page 85
1. Any point whose x value is 0
2. 0
3. x = 3 will be parallel to x = 0 just shifted three units to the right.
4.

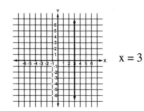

x = 3

5. Shift the line two units to the left.

Predicting Graphs—y = x   **pages 86-87**

1. Any points whose x and y ordinates are equal; for example, (1,1) (-5, -5), and (0,0)

2.

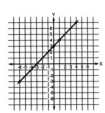

This line is parallel to the line, y = x and crosses the y-axis at 3.

3. This line will be the same as the previous two lines except it will cross the y-axis at 5.

4.

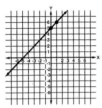

5.

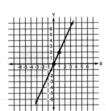

The coefficient changes the slant on the line. The line has a steeper grade.

6.

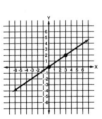

The fractional coefficient results in a line with not as steep of a grade.

7.

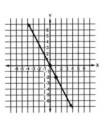

The negative coefficient makes the line slant in the opposite direction. From left to right, this line goes in a downward direction. y = x goes in an upward direction.

8. This line has the same grade of slant as y = ⅔ x but is slanted in the opposite direction.

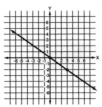

9. This line is very steep, steeper than the line y = 2x. It has a downward slant.

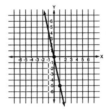

10. This line has an upward slant and is less steep than the line, y = ⅔ x.

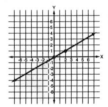

11. This line is the same as the previous line except that it is shifted down two units.

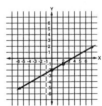